YAS

**FRIENDS
OF ACPL**

Writing the Critical Essay

POLLUTION

An OPPOSING VIEWPOINTS® Guide

Lauri S. Friedman, *Book Editor*

Christine Nasso, *Publisher*
Elizabeth Des Chenes, *Managing Editor*

OPPOSING
VIEWPOINTS®
SERIES

GREENHAVEN PRESS
An imprint of Thomson Gale, a part of The Thomson Corporation

THOMSON
™
GALE

Detroit • New York • San Francisco • New Haven, Conn. • Waterville, Maine • London

THOMSON

GALE

LIBRARY OF CONGRESS CATALOGING-IN-PUBLICATION DATA

Pollution / Lauri S. Friedman, editor.
    p. cm. — (Writing the critical essay)
  Includes bibliographical references and index.
  ISBN-13: 978-0-7377-3198-9 (hardcover)
  1. Pollution. 2. Pollution--Health aspects. 3. Pollution prevention. I. Friedman, Lauri S.
  TD176.7.P63 2007
  363.73—dc22
                                2007032511

ISBN-10: 0-7377-3198-2 (hardcover)
Printed in the United States of America

CONTENTS

Examining the state of writing and how it is taught in the United States was the official purpose of the National Commission on Writing in America's Schools and Colleges. The commission, made up of teachers, school administrators, business leaders, and college and university presidents, released its first report in 2003. "Despite the best efforts of many educators," commissioners argued, "writing has not received the full attention it deserves." Among the findings of the commission was that most fourth-grade students spent less than three hours a week writing, that three-quarters of high school seniors never receive a writing assignment in their history or social studies classes, and that more than 50 percent of first-year students in college have problems writing error-free papers. The commission called for a "cultural sea change" that would increase the emphasis on writing for both elementary and secondary schools. These conclusions have made some educators realize that writing must be emphasized in the curriculum. As colleges are demanding an ever-higher level of writing proficiency from incoming students, schools must respond by making students more competent writers. In response to these concerns, the SAT, an influential standardized test used for college admissions, required an essay for the first time in 2005.

Books in the Writing the Critical Essay: An Opposing Viewpoints Guide series use the patented Opposing Viewpoints format to help students learn to organize ideas and arguments and to write essays using common critical writing techniques. Each book in the series focuses on a particular type of essay writing—including expository, persuasive, descriptive, and narrative—that students learn while being taught both the five-paragraph essay as well as longer pieces of writing that have an opinionated focus. These guides include everything necessary to help students research, outline, draft, edit, and ultimately write successful essays across the curriculum, including essays for the SAT.

Using Opposing Viewpoints

This series is inspired by and builds upon Greenhaven Press's acclaimed Opposing Viewpoints series. As in the parent series, each book in the Writing the Critical Essay series focuses on a timely and controversial social issue that provides lots of opportunities for creating thought-provoking essays. The first section of each volume begins with a brief introductory essay that provides context for the opposing viewpoints that follow. These articles are chosen for their accessibility and clearly stated views. The thesis of each article is made explicit in the article's title and is accentuated by its pairing with an opposing or alternative view. These essays are both models of persuasive writing techniques and valuable research material that students can mine to write their own informed essays. Guided reading and discussion questions help lead students to key ideas and writing techniques presented in the selections.

The second section of each book begins with a preface discussing the format of the essays and examining characteristics of the featured essay type. Model five-paragraph and longer essays then demonstrate that essay type. The essays are annotated so that key writing elements and techniques are pointed out to the student. Sequential, step-by-step exercises help students construct and refine thesis statements; organize material into outlines; analyze and try out writing techniques; write transitions, introductions, and conclusions; and incorporate quotations and other researched material. Ultimately, students construct their own compositions using the designated essay type.

The third section of each volume provides additional research material and writing prompts to help the student. Additional facts about the topic of the book serve as a convenient source of supporting material for essays. Other features help students go beyond the book for their research. Like other Greenhaven Press books, each book in the Writing the Critical Essay series includes bibliographic listings of relevant periodical articles, books, Web sites, and organizations to contact.

Writing the Critical Essay: An Opposing Viewpoints Guide will help students master essay techniques that can be used in any discipline.

Disposing Our Disposable Culture

Americans are frequently chided for having a "throw-it-away" consumer culture, meaning that they tend to favor products that are cheap and disposable. This culture has resulted in the United States holding the global record for the most trash produced, an astonishing fact when one considers the United States is home to just 5 percent of the global population. This means that 5 percent of the world's people generate 40 percent of its waste—a legacy that few Americans are proud of.

According to the Environmental Protection Agency, the average American throws away 4.5 pounds of trash a day, and the nation produces more than 230 million tons of waste annually. Put another way, Americans throw away enough trash to fill 63,000 garbage trucks a day. Over the course of one year, America's trash would fill enough garbage trucks to form a line stretching from Earth halfway to the moon, or to form a line long enough to wrap nearly five times around Earth—a distance of more than 119,000 miles!

One reason America is such a trash-making country is its affluence. As incomes rose throughout the twentieth century, so did the demand for more goods. These goods traveled farther from manufacturer to shelf, requiring more packaging to protect them along their journey. As more people around the country saw their incomes rise, they too could afford pricey consumer goods and gadgets, which meant more were produced, along with more packaging. Increased income also led many Americans to opt for a more convenient product, which is often one that is used once and thrown away.

America's wealth affected its consumer culture in another important way. It encouraged people to buy new items

Kentucky Governor Paul Patton speaks at a metal waste disposal site on the importance of reducing waste and recycling.

whenever their possessions broke, rather than having them fixed. Instead of spending money and time fixing an older, broken item, oftentimes it seems more convenient to throw it out and buy a new one at a nearby store (and usually for not much more money than it would cost to fix the broken item). Indeed, in most American cities, repair shops are rare, and if they exist, they are seldom used. As writer Vernon Stent notes, "In affluent countries those days [of fixing items] are gone, taking with them the watch repairer, the radio (and TV) repair man, the cobbler, etc. Even replacing the battery in an electric wrist watch is often virtually impossible."[1]

Together these factors led to the development of a "disposable culture," one in which it is easier and cheaper to throw an item away and to replace it by purchasing a new item. Some regard the throw-away consumer mentality as American as apple pie. Writes author Elizabeth Grossman, "What could be more American than reaching for something new? The U.S. is, after all, a nation founded on the rejection of tradition and a profound belief in invention. This urge has given us more than two centuries of powerful technology, but has also made Americans the world's most voracious consumers."[2]

But Americans, and the rest of the world, are beginning to pay the price for such a lifestyle. Trash pollution is on the rise, and more of the world's landfills are becoming filled to capacity. In the twenty-first century, therefore, increasing numbers of Americans are beginning to take part in a recycling movement that not only finds new uses for old products, but also encourages less packaging, or packaging made out of recycled materials. Incredibly, about one-third of the waste generated in America is due to packaging. Therefore, cutting down on consumer packaging is one way to reduce pollution. Companies have made efforts to appear "green" or "eco-friendly" by cutting out the materials in which they package their product. Examples are DVDs and CDs. Such products used to be accompanied by bulky plastic packaging that more than tripled the weight and size of the disk it protected. The modern approach is to use sleek, small packaging made from nonplastic materials, even recycled cardboard (the popular movie *An Inconvenient Truth*, for

---

[1] Vernon Stent, "Throwing Away the Throw-Away Culture," EzineArticles, September 7, 2005. http://ezinearticles.com/?Throwing-Away-the-Throw-Away-Culture&id = 69046.
[2] Elizabeth Grossman, "Them's the Breaks," Grist.com, June 29, 2006. www.grist. org/advice/books/2006/06/29/grossman.

example, was sold in minimalist packaging to underscore the documentary's point that Americans need to conserve their resources).

Minimalist packaging and recycling can go a long way toward reducing pollution from trash. According to the National Recycling Coalition, the Environmental Protection Agency, and Earth911.org, modern recycling techniques are so effective that a used aluminum can is recycled and back on the grocery shelf in a new form in under sixty days. Recycling one aluminum can saves enough energy to run a TV for three hours—or the equivalent of a half a gallon of gasoline. Furthermore, recycling that aluminum can saves 96 percent of the energy used to make a new can, and also produces 95 percent less air pollution and 97 percent less water pollution. For these reasons, recycling continues to be a critical way of reducing trash, water, and air pollution. This is especially noteworthy considering that when an aluminum can is not recycled, it will take more than 500 years to naturally decompose. When one thinks about how more than 80 billion aluminum soda cans are used every year, the environmental impact recycling can have is astonishing.

Recycling is one of the many efforts that can be used to prevent and reduce pollution in the United States. As the environment becomes an increasingly relevant topic, ways to reduce pollution will also become popular and critical to study. To this end, the articles and model essays included in *Writing the Critical Essay: An Opposing Viewpoints Guide: Pollution* expose readers to the basic arguments made about pollution and help them develop tools to craft their own essays on the subject.

Recycling receptacles—like this one at a New Jersey Turnpike service area—are an increasingly common sight as the public has become more concerned about pollution.

Section One:
Opposing
Viewpoints
on Pollution

Air Pollution Is a Serious Problem

Supryia Ray

In the following viewpoint, author Supryia Ray presents data that indicates air pollution in America is a serious problem and is getting worse. In 2004, for example, fine particle pollution (a sooty pollution that causes serious health problems) exceeded the national health standards in twenty-one states, affecting the health of 96 million people. Ray argues that even if air pollution was at national health standard levels, the levels are too low to sufficiently protect health. Ray concludes that national air pollution standards must be improved and enforced by lawmakers and politicians.

Supryia Ray is a clean air advocate with the U.S. Public Interest Research Group (U.S. PIRG) Education Fund, a national organization that advocates improving the environment.

Consider the Following Questions:

1. Name four health effects of air pollution, as presented by the author.
2. What California region had the worst annual fine particle pollution of any metropolitan area, according to the author?
3. According to the author, how many deaths occur each year from fine particle pollution produced by power plants?

While air quality has improved in the U.S. since the inception of the Clean Air Act in 1970, more than 88 million Americans still live in areas with unsafe levels of fine particle pollution. Fine particle pollution is one of the nation's most pervasive air pollutants and its most deadly, causing tens of thousands of premature deaths every year. This report examines levels of fine particle pollution in cities and towns nationwide in 2004 and finds that fine particles continue to pose a grave health threat to Americans.

Pollution and Health

Fine particle, or "soot," pollution can cause serious respiratory and cardiovascular problems, including asthma attacks, heart attacks, strokes, lung cancer, and premature death. Moreover, recent scientific studies show that such adverse effects occur at levels below the current national health-based air quality standards, which include an annual standard of 15 micrograms per cubic meter ($\mu g/m^3$) and a daily standard of 65 $\mu g/m^3$. Combustion sources such as coal-fired power plants and diesel engines are the largest source of fine particle pollution.

This report is based on a compilation of 2004 data from the nation's network of fine particle air quality monitors, as detailed by the state environmental agencies we surveyed. . . .

Pollution Exceeds Standards Across the Board

- In 2004, fine particle pollution exceeded the annual and/or daily national health standard at air quality monitors in 55 small, mid-sized, and large metropolitan areas located in 21 states and home to 96 million people. States with exceedances of both standards included California, Georgia, Pennsylvania, and Utah.
- In 2004, fine particle pollution exceeded the annual national health standard in 43 metropolitan areas crossing 21 states' borders. Riverside–San Bernardino–Ontario, a large metropolitan area in California, had the

worst annual fine particle pollution of any metropolitan area, with a maximum average annual level nearly 50 percent higher than the health standard. Among mid-sized and small metropolitan areas, Bakersfield and the Hanford-Corcoran areas in California had the worst annual fine particle pollution.

- In 2004, fine particle pollution exceeded the daily national health standard in 20 metropolitan areas crossing 10 states' borders. Fine particle pollution in these areas spiked above the standard 92 times on 45 days.

While hiking in the Blue Ridge Mountains near Asheville, North Carolina, Bill Jackson, a U.S. Forest Service air resource specialist, talks about air pollution in the Southeast's national parks.

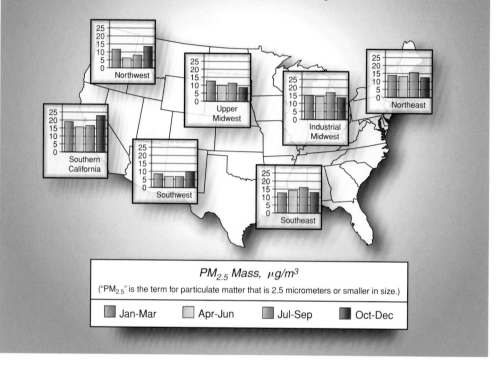

Seasonal Averages of Fine Particle Pollution

In the West, fine particle pollution tends to be higher in the winter months. In the East, it tends to be higher during the summer.

PM$_{2.5}$ Mass, $\mu g/m^3$

("PM$_{2.5}$" is the term for particulate matter that is 2.5 micrometers or smaller in size.)

■ Jan-Mar   ☐ Apr-Jun   ■ Jul-Sep   ■ Oct-Dec

Areas Across the Country Suffering

- Among the states, Utah suffered the most spikes in fine particle pollution due to a winter-time temperature inversion, with 47 exceedances of the daily standard on 18 days in January and February of 2004. California experienced spikes in fine particle pollution on 16 days, recording 30 exceedances in cities and towns across the state.

- Of the largest metropolitan areas, Pittsburgh, Pennsylvania experienced the most days with spikes in fine particle pollution, recording seven exceedances on seven different days. The Riverside–San Bernardino–Ontario metropolitan area in California ranked second among the largest metropolitan areas, recording 14 exceedances on six different days.

- Logan, a small metropolitan area on the border of Utah and Idaho, suffered the most spikes in fine particle pollution of any metropolitan area in the country—17 exceedances on 17 days. The Logan metropolitan area also recorded one of the highest exceedances in 2004, a maximum spike of 132.8, more than double the health standard.

Clean Air Laws Must Be Enforced

Unfortunately, the Clean Air Act's New Source Review program, which is critical to reducing fine particle pollution from aging power plants, continues to come under attack. A recent analysis found that eliminating the program would cut short the lives of 70,000 Americans in the next two decades, as a result of higher levels of fine particle pollution in the air than current law permits. Policymakers should reject weakening changes to the program and instead enforce the law.

Rather than take additional steps to further limit levels of fine particle pollution in our air, however, the [President George W.] Bush administration recently proposed to maintain the status quo. Under the Clean Air Act, the Environmental Protection Agency (EPA) must set air quality standards at levels that protect public health, including the health of sensitive populations, with an adequate margin of safety. EPA also must review the standards every five years to ensure they reflect the latest scientific knowledge and update the standards as needed.

Current Standards Do Not Protect Health

EPA staff scientists and the Clean Air Scientific Advisory Committee, an independent review committee, separately concluded in 2005 that the current standards do not adequately protect public health and recommended substantially strengthening the standards. The Bush administration, however, disregarded the advice of these experts, proposing in December 2005 to maintain the annual health standard of

Rush hour traffic in Portland, Oregon. Motor vehicles play a major role in air pollution.

15 μg/m^3 and slightly lower the daily health standard from 65 μg/m^3 to 35 μg/m^3.

Given the extent of fine particle pollution in the U.S. and the science showing serious adverse health effects below the current fine particle standards, the Bush administration should adopt an annual standard no higher than 12 μg/m^3 and a daily standard no higher than 25 μg/m^3 when it finalizes the standards in September 2006. . . .

Health Effects of Fine Particle Pollution

Both coarse particles and fine particles are associated with serious respiratory and cardiovascular problems. With respect to fine particles—the focus of this report—EPA has concluded that "[t]he health effects associated with exposure to $PM_{2.5}$ are significant." As the agency explains, "[e]pidemiological studies have shown a significant correlation between elevated $PM_{2.5}$ levels and premature mortality. Other important effects associated with $PM_{2.5}$ exposure include aggravation of respiratory and cardiovascular disease . . . lung disease, decreased lung function, asthma attacks, and certain cardiovascular problems."

Notably, both short-term and long-term exposure to fine particles can cause premature death. Numerous studies have linked fine particle exposure to premature death, and EPA has estimated that particle pollution shortens the lives of its victims by an average of 14 years. Indeed, agency scientists recently estimated that, even at the level of current air quality standards for fine particles, fine particle pollution causes more than 4,700 premature deaths each year in just nine cities: Detroit, Los Angeles, Philadelphia, Pittsburgh, St. Louis, Phoenix, Seattle, and San Jose. Moreover, a 2004 study by Abt Associates, EPA's air quality consultants, found that fine particles from U.S. power plants alone cause 23,600 premature deaths per year, in addition to 38,200 non-fatal heart attacks and 554,000 asthma attacks.

Serious Illness and Death

Likewise, both short-term and long-term exposure to fine particles can cause serious illness. Adverse impacts of short-term increases in fine particle pollution include non-fatal heart attacks, especially among the elderly and people with heart conditions; hospitalization for cardiovascular disease, including strokes; emergency room visits for acute respiratory ailments; inflammation of lung tissue in young, healthy adults; hospitalization for asthma among children; and severe asthma attacks in children. Adverse impacts of long-term (chronic) exposure to fine particle pollution include significant damage to the small airways of the lungs, slowed lung function growth in children and teens, and hospitalization for asthma attacks among children who live near roads with heavy truck or trailer traffic. Moreover, long-term exposure to fine particle pollution also is associated with premature births even at low levels.

Groups at greatest risk from fine particle pollution include older adults, people with heart or lung disease, and children. Recent research indicates that diabetics are also at increased risk from fine particle pollution. . . .

We Must Do Better

As this report shows, metropolitan areas of all sizes across the country continue to struggle with fine particle pollution. Since the air quality standards for fine particle pollution were adopted in 1997, thousands of peer-reviewed studies have reaffirmed that exposure to fine particles can cause serious health effects, even at levels well below the current standards.

Air Pollution Is Making Us Sick

Not only can that black plume of smoke from the tailpipe or the graying haze settling over the city make you cough and blink, but it can do much worse—it could help take months to years off of your life. . . . Analyses undertaken over the past five years tie air pollution to shorter lives, heart disease, lung cancer, asthma attacks, and serious interference with the growth and work of the lungs..

American Lung Association, "Health Effects of Ozone and Particle Pollution." In *State of the Air* 2005.

Analyze the Essay:

1. Supryia Ray relies on an extensive amount of data to argue that air pollution is a serious threat to Americans' health. Where does this data come from? In your opinion, is it authoritative?
2. What agencies, experts, or other voices were quoted in Ray's essay? In what way were these voices used to bolster the author's argument?

The Problem of Air Pollution Has Been Exaggerated

Joel Schwartz

In the following viewpoint, author Joel Schwartz argues air pollution is no longer a serious problem in America. He cites data showing that the quality of America's air has steadily improved since 1980. But Americans believe air pollution is still a problem, according to Schwartz, because they are mislead by media and environmental sources that seek to sensationalize the problem. Most reports about air pollution are either overblown or misleading, in Schwartz's view. He concludes that federal regulation is not necessary in order to continue improving the state of the nation's air—it is an unnecessary oversight that wastes federal tax dollars.

Joel Schwartz is a visiting fellow at the American Enterprise Institute, where he studies air pollution, transportation, climate change, and chemical risks. He has authored numerous studies on air pollution trends, control strategies, health effects, and regulatory policy, including this piece that was published by the National Center for Policy Analysis.

Consider the Following Questions:

1. According to the author, how much did fine particulate matter decline between 1980 and 2005?
2. Why does the author take issue with a claim by *USA Today* that American vehicles pollute more today than in the 1980s?
3. What are three examples the author gives to argue that federal pollution regulations are unnecessary?

Joel Schwartz, "Facts Not Fear on Air Pollution," NCPA Policy Report No. 294, National Center for Policy Analysis, December 2006, pp. 1, 5–7, 15–16, 22–23.

ost of what Americans "know" about air pollution is
false. Polls show most Americans believe air pollution
has been steady or rising during the last few decades and
will worsen in the future, and is a serious threat to people's
health. But these widely held views are based on myths
that are demonstrably false. Air quality in America's cities
is better than it has been in more than a century, despite
the fact that Americans are driving more miles, using more
energy, and producing and consuming more goods and services than ever. . . .

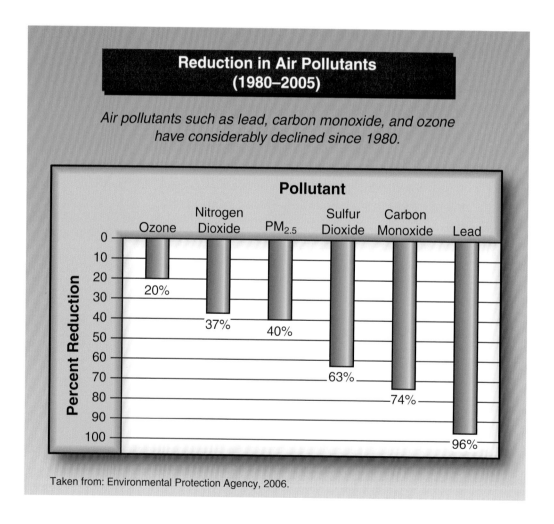

Reduction in Air Pollutants (1980–2005)

Air pollutants such as lead, carbon monoxide, and ozone have considerably declined since 1980.

Taken from: Environmental Protection Agency, 2006.

Air Quality Has Improved

Air pollution has been declining for decades across the United States. Since the passage of the Clean Air Act in 1970, the U.S. Environmental Protection Agency (EPA) has been the federal agency charged with monitoring and regulating emissions of air pollutants. . . . Between 1980 and 2005:

- Fine particulate matter ($PM_{2.5}$) declined 40 percent.
- Peak 8-hour ozone (O_3) levels declined 20 percent, and days per year exceeding the 8-hour ozone standard fell 79 percent.
- The improvement was even greater for the older, less stringent 1-hour ozone standard; peak levels dropped 28 percent and exceedances days dropped 94 percent.
- Nitrogen dioxide (NO_2) concentrations in air dropped 37 percent while sulfur dioxide (SO_2) decreased 63 percent; carbon monoxide (CO) levels dropped 74 percent; and lead declined 96 percent. . . .

Widespread Misinformation

While air pollution levels have declined, polls show most Americans think air pollution has stayed the same or even increased and will continue to increase in the future. The reason: Most information on air pollution from environmentalists, regulators and journalists—the public's main sources for information on the environment—is false. Here are just a few examples:

- In November 2001, the Sierra Club wrote that "smog is out of control in almost all of our major cities"—after two years of the lowest recorded levels of ozone and fine particulates ($PM_{2.5}$) nationwide.
- In 2002, the Public Interest Research Group published *Darkening Skies*, which claimed $PM_{2.5}$ was increasing—near the end of a fourth consecutive record-low year for $PM_{2.5}$.

A senior air pollution specialist with the Minnesota Pollution Control Agency demonstrates a machine used to monitor the amount of fine particulate matter pollution in the air.

- In April 2004, the *Washington Post* lamented, "Ozone pollution has declined *slightly* over the past 30 years" (emphasis added)—although, nationwide, the total number of times the l-hour and 8-hour ozone standards were exceeded had declined 95 percent and 65 percent, respectively, since the mid-1970s.
- A recent *USA Today* article claimed Americans now drive "vehicles that give off more pollution than the cars they drove in the '80s"—despite spectacular improvements in automobile emissions performance during the last few decades.

Exaggerations and Lack of Context

Similarly, in December 2005, EPA proposed a lower 24-hour standard for fine particulates ($PM_{2.5}$) that would nearly double the number of areas violating the federal standard. Yet activists and journalists created the impression that the EPA had not tightened the standard at all. "EPA proposes 'Status Quo' revisions to PM NAAQS [particulate matter standard]," claimed an American Lung Association press release. According to Clean Air Watch, another environmental group, "President Bush gives early Christmas present to smokestack industries." The *Atlanta Journal-Constitution* headline read, "EPA Barely Budges on Soot; Health Advice Disregarded." . . .

These exaggerations mislead tens of millions of Americans into believing their air is far more polluted and dangerous than it really is. The lack of temporal context adds to the misperception. Someplace in the United States has to be the worst at any given time. But even in the

> ## Our Air Is Cleaner than Ever
>
> Every category of air pollution has fallen during the [President George W.] Bush years, with 2003, 2004, and 2005 showing the lowest levels of harmful ozone and particulates in the air since the monitoring of air pollution began in the 1960s. . . . Reducing air pollution has been the single greatest environmental-policy success of our time. Emissions are falling fast, and are going to keep falling. Despite more cars on the road and more drivers per capita, automobile emissions are falling 8 percent a year, and EPA [Environmental Protection Agency] models predict a further 80-percent reduction in car and truck emissions over the next 20 years.
>
> *National Review* "Polluted Thinking," July 25, 2006.

"worst" areas of the country, air pollution is much lower now than it used to be. For example, Riverside, Calif., has the highest $PM_{2.5}$ levels in the country. But $PM_{2.5}$ in Riverside has dropped more than 50 percent since the early 1980s. Ignoring and obscuring these large improvements widens the gap between public perception and actual air quality.
. . .

Federal Air Regulations Hurt America

The Clean Air Act and federal regulation were not *necessary* to reduce air pollution. Air pollution has indeed sharply declined since the Clean Air Act was adopted. But regulators and environmentalists create the false impression that air pollution was on an ever-rising trajectory before the federal government stepped in to protect Americans from unrestrained capitalism and from state and local governments more interested in jobs and economic growth than their citizens' health. This self-serving picture is false. Air pollution had been dropping for decades before the federal government took over policy control in 1970. For example:

- Pittsburgh reduced particulate levels by more than 75 percent between the early 1900s and 1970.
- Chicago, Cincinnati and New York all have records going back to the 1930s or 1940s showing ongoing reductions in particulate matter leading up to the Clean Air Act.
- Los Angeles began reducing ozone in the 1950s, soon after sky-rocketing population and automobile use created the problem; ozone has been declining ever since.
- Between 1960 and 1970, total suspended particulate levels declined nearly 20 percent nationwide, while average sulfur dioxide levels dropped 36 percent— nearly 60 percent in New York City.

Through a combination of market forces pressing for greater energy efficiency and cleaner technologies, common-law nuisance suits, and local and state regulation, Americans were addressing air pollution decades before the federal government took over policy control. Air pollution is not unique in this respect. Other environmental problems, such as water quality, were also improving before the federal government took over.

A chemist with the South Coast Air Quality Management District compares filters from fine particulate matter detectors stationed in Los Angeles (left) and Lynwood (right), California.

The Price of Clean Air Regulations

If air pollution could be reduced for free we could be less concerned about the validity of alarming claims of harm from low-level air pollution. But reducing air pollution is costly. Attaining the federal 8-hour ozone and annual $PM_{2.5}$ standards will cost tens to hundreds of billions of dollars per year. These costs are ultimately paid by people in the form of higher prices, lower wages and reduced choices. Spending more on air quality means spending less on other things that improve health, safety and welfare. . . .

Let's Use Our Money to Fight More Serious Problems

Virtually everyone would agree that we need clean air and that people have a right to be free from unreasonable risks imposed by others. But current air pollution standards are already more than stringent enough to protect people's health. Regulatory programs are cloaked in the language of public health. But they are really about protecting and expanding the powers of federal and state regulators, creating competitive advantage for businesses that can effectively work the system, and allowing environmental activists to override people's preferences and impose their own values regarding how Americans ought to live, work and travel.

Americans need and deserve an air quality regulatory system that is narrowly tailored to solve real problems, rather than used to expand and perpetuate the power of government bureaucracies, environmental activists and other special interests. The first step to achieving this goal is more realistic public information about air pollution levels, trends and, especially, health risks, as well as greater public understanding that regulators and environmental activists are special interests in the same way as other participants in regulatory policy debates, and that they often pursue policies that are at odds with the interests and values of most Americans.

Journalists have so far failed to turn a critical eye on our air pollution regulatory system or to look beneath the surface of activists' and regulators' press releases. Yet among the major providers of public information on the environment, reporters are in the best position to turn the tide of misinformation on air pollution. It would be a breath of fresh air if they took up this challenge.

Analyze the Essay:

1. One of Joel Schwartz's main points is that Americans have been misled by environmentalists and journalists. Why does Schwartz believe this? After summarizing his argument, explain whether you think his idea is plausible or not.

2. Both Joel Schwartz and the author of the previous viewpoint, Supryia Ray, note that the Riverside, California, area has the highest fine particle pollution in the nation. Yet in what way do they differ in their assessments of Riverside's pollution problem? Explain how each author uses the Riverside data in the context of his or her argument.

Water Pollution Is a Serious Problem

Alex Markels and Randy Dotinga

In the following viewpoint, authors Alex Markels and Randy Dotinga discuss how water pollution is a serious problem that sickens thousands of people every year. Indeed, say the authors, thousands of beaches must post advisories warning people against getting in the water for fear of contracting dangerous bacteria that can lead to sickness and even death. Such pollution comes from outdated sewage systems, over-run septic systems, pesticide runoff, and other waste that finds its way to a nearby water source. The authors conclude that stricter monitoring systems and improved testing systems must be put into place in order to protect America's recreational areas.

Alex Markels is a Ted Scripps fellow at the University of Colorado's Center for Environmental Journalism. Randy Dotinga is a freelance medical and crime reporter.

Consider the Following Questions:

1. What health problems did Nadia Starner's kids experience after swimming in polluted water, as reported by the authors?
2. Why are "baby" or "kiddie" beaches typically more contaminated than other beaches, according to the authors?
3. According to the authors, what is the problem with current testing methods for fecal bacteria and E. coli?

Alex Markels and Randy Dotinga, "Don't go in the water," *U.S. News & World Report*, vol. 137, August 16, 2004, p. 74. Copyright © 2004 *U.S. News & World Report*, L.P. All rights reserved. Reprinted with permission.

It should have been a carefree day at the beach. But despite the cloudless sky, the blue ocean, and the soft sands along California's Doheny State Beach, signs warning swimmers that BACTERIA LEVELS HAVE EXCEEDED STATE STANDARDS forced Nadia Starner to sit her children down for a serious talk.

"You can put your feet in, but no splashing," she told Kyle, 12, and Makena, 10, as they prepared to launch their kayaks from the shore of Baby Beach, a harborside stretch preferred by local families as a safe, wave-free area. "And don't dunk your head under the water!"

But it wasn't long before the admonishments faded and the fun began. Inevitably, the kayaks tipped, the water

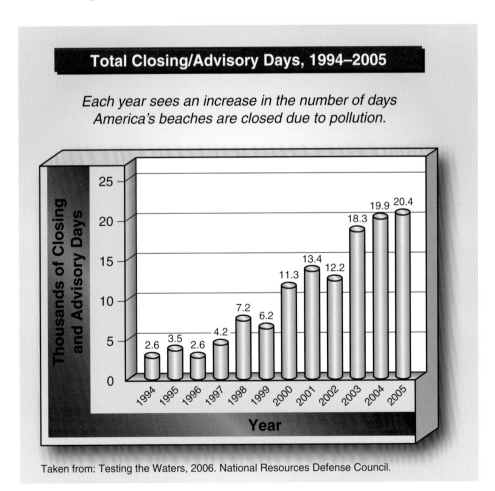

Total Closing/Advisory Days, 1994–2005

Each year sees an increase in the number of days America's beaches are closed due to pollution.

Taken from: Testing the Waters, 2006. National Resources Defense Council.

A sign warns visitors to California's Doheny State Beach that the ocean water there contains unsafe levels of bacteria.

splashed, and Starner shrugged. "It's hard to tell a child, 'Don't get wet!' when you go to the beach," she says.

Water Pollution Has Serious Consequences

Even harder was hearing her kids complain later of stomach-aches, as fecal bacteria from a nearby creek had fouled the beach water, then found its way into Kyle's and Makena's mouths. When Makena started throwing up in the middle of the night, "that was it," Starner says. She decided to keep her kids from swimming at the beach ever again.

The Starners aren't the only ones being forced to abandon their favorite beaches. From sewage spills off Los Angeles

2005 Beach Closing/Advisories and Monitoring Programs

Guam Northern Mariana Islands Puerto Rico U.S. Virgin Islands

Complete monitoring: All reported beaches are monitored at least once a month

Limited monitoring: Fewer than half the reported beaches are monitored at least once a month

Extensive monitoring: More than half the reported beaches are monitored at least once a month

States not included in study

Taken from: Testing the Waters 2006, Natural Resources Defence Council

and Milwaukee to unexplained algae blooms near Virginia's Colonial Beach and dangerous levels of bacteria along seashores in Rhode Island, North Carolina, Florida, and Washington, water pollution has closed scores of beaches so far this summer [2004]. Thousands more have posted advisories warning against swimming.

"The Pollution Just Sits There"

Ironically, protected beaches like the one where Starner's children got sick are among the worst. "If it's called 'baby' or 'kiddie' beach, chances are that it's going to pose an elevated health risk," says Mark Gold, an environmental scientist who heads California's Heal the Bay, a nonprofit group that recently dubbed Doheny California's worst "beach bummer." "Yes, the risk of drowning is substantially less at those beaches," Gold says. "But because they're enclosed and often near storm drains, the water stagnates and the pollution just sits there."

Those who swim in tainted waters risk gastrointestinal illnesses that can cause nausea, vomiting, and diarrhea, as well as sinus and upper respiratory infections. Swallowing bad water is usually to blame. But even skin contact can produce rashes, swimmer's ear, and infections of open wounds. Although most beach-related illnesses aren't life threatening, swimmers and surfers have sometimes been stricken by serious viruses. "We've had a couple of cases of possible viral myocarditis," says Jeffrey Harris, a Malibu, Calif., physician who has treated local surfers for the dangerous inflammation of the heart muscle. "One guy had to have multiple heart transplants and eventually died."

Eighteen Thousand Unhealthy Days

Levels of overall contamination have most likely remained fairly constant in recent years, experts say. Yet the number of closures and advisories has skyrocketed, thanks largely to increased water quality testing. This summer's numbers could surpass those logged in 2003, when the nation's beaches suffered more than 18,000 unhealthy days—a 50 percent increase over the previous year, according to the Natural Resources Defense Council. "This is a huge problem that we simply used to ignore," says Nancy Stoner, director of the NRDC's Clean Water Project, whose annual report is based on statistics gathered by the U.S. Environmental Protection Agency. "People would get sick after going to the beach. But without monitoring and warning signs, they wouldn't know why."

In most cases, the exact sources of the pollution are unknown. Yet the broader causes make up a laundry list of urban ills: aging, overrun sewage treatment and septic systems; runoff from irrigated fields and lawns doused with fertilizer and pesticides; and storm water runoff from streets and rooftops caked with sediment, motor oil, and animal waste.

We Need Tougher Regulations

Then, of course, there are the debilitating effects of development on Mother Nature's kidneys: the wetlands that absorb runoff and filter out contaminants before they can reach rivers, lakes, and oceans. Unlike "point source" pollution, long regulated by the EPA, such as direct discharges of effluent from industrial plants, there is little federal oversight of nonpoint pollution.

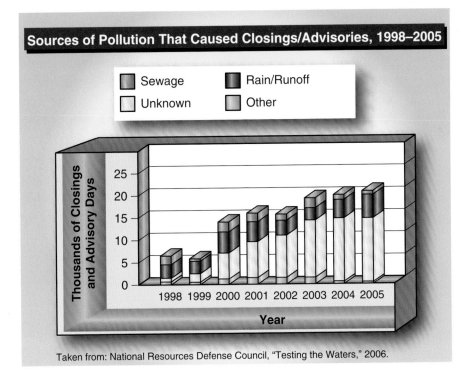

Sources of Pollution That Caused Closings/Advisories, 1998–2005

Taken from: National Resources Defense Council, "Testing the Waters," 2006.

People who are frequently in the water—like these Huntington Beach, California, surfers—are especially vulnerable to waterborne diseases.

Gold and other activists say regulations on storm water runoff aren't nearly as tough as they should be, while treatment of agricultural runoff is largely voluntary.

For their part, EPA administrators say there is little that can be done without first knowing the precise sources of the pollution. So they have focused on improving testing. The BEACH Act of 2000 requires states to adopt minimum water quality standards, improve monitoring, and issue warnings about pollution. The EPA recently announced that it would force 25 states that have yet to adopt its standards to do so by the end of the year. And it has launched a website listing water quality conditions at thousands of beaches nationwide.

Abandoning the Beaches

Yet even with better monitoring, it's often a crapshoot whether the postings accurately reflect current conditions. That's largely because standard tests for fecal bacteria and E. coli take up to three days to yield results, "which is a lot like trying to navigate the freeways using traffic information that's two or three days old," says Stanley Grant, a professor of environmental engineering at the University of California-Irvine.

In a recent study, Grant compared warning signs posted along Huntington Beach, Calif., with records of actual water quality there and found the signs were wrong up to 40 percent of the time. With plumes of contaminated water mixing with fast-moving currents, "you pretty much need a stoplight in the water to know whether it's safe to go in," says Grant. EPA scientists say that should change as new DNA-based tests cut the turnaround time for results from a few days to a few hours.

All that is little consolation to people like Nadia Starner and her children, who have all but abandoned the beach this summer. "There are a lot of beaches where they don't have warning signs posted, but my kids still come home sick sometimes," she says. "So now we're looking for friends who have swimming pools."

Analyze the Essay:

1. Alex Markels and Randy Dotinga personalize the problem of water pollution by focusing on the Starner family's experience with water pollution. What do you think of this technique? Did it draw you into the story? Did you find it an effective tool for discussing the problem? Why or why not?

2. Examine what authorities, experts, or agencies were quoted in this viewpoint. Where were these quotes used, and how effective were they? Cite evidence from the text in your answer.

The Problem of Water Pollution Has Been Exaggerated

G. Tracy Mehan III

In the following viewpoint, author G. Tracy Mehan III argues that water pollution is declining. He discusses a report on the Great Lakes which concludes that toxic chemicals and other pollutants in the water are declining thanks to massive clean-up efforts supported by both the United States and Canada. In part, claims Mehan, this is because many airborne pollutants that find their way to water have been reduced. Mehan applauds the United States and Canada for making great gains in cleaning up both their air and water, and advises Americans not to be scared by negative news they hear about the environment, for the world is much cleaner than they are usually told.

G. Tracy Mehan III was assistant administrator for water at the Environmental Protection Agency and director of the Michigan Office of the Great Lakes, serving in the cabinet of Governor John Engler. Presently, he is a consultant with the Cadmus Group, Inc., an environmental consulting firm.

Consider the Following Questions:

1. According to the author, what priority pollutants are being successfully removed from the Great Lakes?
2. Name four products that no longer contain mercury, according to the author.
3. What is a top priority of the Binational Toxics Strategy, as reported by the author?

The U.S. Environmental Protection Agency (EPA) and Environment Canada are poised to highlight more good news on North America's environment.

The 2004 Annual Progress Report on the Great Lakes Binational Toxics Strategy, just off the press but, as of this writing, not yet released, documents progress in dealing with a particularly nasty suite of persistent, toxic chemicals which accumulate in the environment with increasing concentration up the food web. These are pollutants of national and international concern, but they have pronounced impacts on the biota and fisheries of the Great Lakes, and the people who rely on them, because of the size of the lakes and the

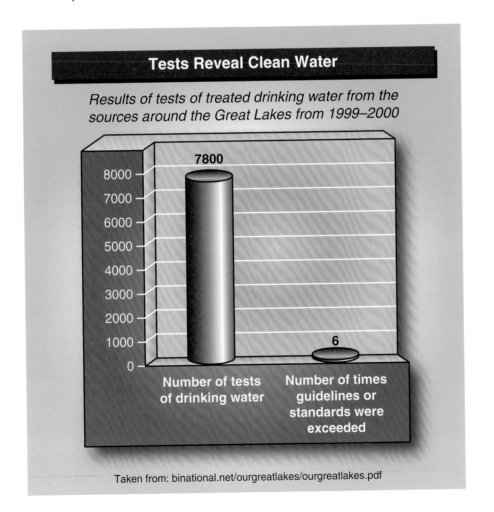

Tests Reveal Clean Water

Results of tests of treated drinking water from the sources around the Great Lakes from 1999–2000

Taken from: binational.net/ourgreatlakes/ourgreatlakes.pdf

At a pollution cleanup project near Seattle, site manager Cliff Leeper holds up jars showing water from the site before and after cleaning treatments.

longer residence time of the contaminants in such huge bodies of water.

The strategy was the result of a 1997 agreement between the U.S. and Canada to virtually eliminate toxic substances from the Great Lakes to meet previous commitments under their Great Lakes Water Quality Agreement. As ambitious or foolhardy as this goal may sound, it seems that success is within reach with respect to priority pollutants such as mercury, PCBs, dioxins/furans, and hexechlorobenzene (HCB).

A Snapshot of Tremendous Progress

Using "Great Lakes" in the title is somewhat confusing since the goals for both countries are, for the most part, national in scope. But these waters are major receptors of the pollutants addressed in the Strategy. Many of these pollutants travel great distances in the air. In the case of some, mercury for instance, they cycle about globally. Nevertheless, the 2004 report gives us a snapshot of tremendous progress which extends well beyond just the Great Lakes region.

Of the 17 reduction goals set forth for the top twelve toxic substances ("Level 1") back in 1997, "ten have been met, three will be met by the target timeline date of 2006, and the remaining four will be well advanced toward, meeting the targets by 2006," states the report.

Mercury Levels Are Down

Regarding mercury, the subject of much debate in Washington these days, the report notes that the U.S. met its national mercury-use reduction goal of 50 percent, and currently stands at over 50 percent based on a 1990 baseline. Mercury is now out of batteries, paints, high-school labs, some illuminated tennis shoes, and other products. When was the last time your kids played with elemental mercury in the high-school chemistry lab? Digital thermometers obviate the need for mercury in that high-volume product, too. In the mid-1990s, this writer, on behalf of then Governor John Engler of Michigan, worked with the Big Three auto companies to phase out 9.8 metric tons of mercury going into convenience-light switches under hoods and trunks annually. The chlor-alkali industry accounted for almost 35 percent of mercury use in 1995, and its total mercury use decreased 76 percent between 1995 and 2003 (with some plant closures). The fluorescent-lamp

Clean Freshwater Abounds

[The] remarkable progress in water quality, achieved in just a few decades by the United States and by other affluent countries, provides grounds for optimism regarding the possibility of bringing high-quality water supplies to people everywhere. The world's freshwater supply is plentiful, more than adequate to sustain a healthy life for nine billion or more people. In the coming decades technological innovations will potentially increase both water quality and efficient water use.

Jack M. Hollander, "Water, Water Everywhere." In *The Real Environmental Crisis: Why Poverty, Not Affluence, Is The Environment's Number One Enemy.* Berkeley: University of California Press, 2004.

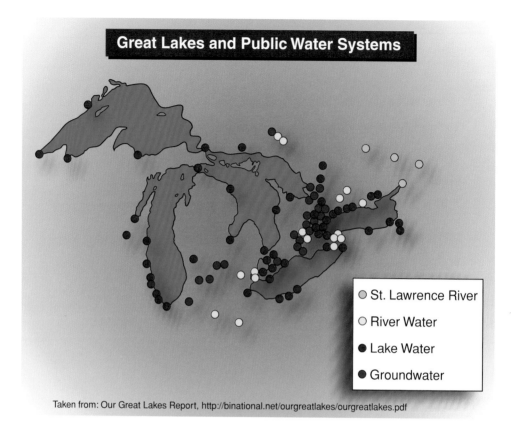

Great Lakes and Public Water Systems

- ○ St. Lawrence River
- ○ River Water
- ● Lake Water
- ● Groundwater

Taken from: Our Great Lakes Report, http://binational.net/ourgreatlakes/ourgreatlakes.pdf

industry reported using 6 tons of mercury in 2003, down from 32 tons in 1997.

The Canadians are also making great progress towards a 90-percent reduction goal (based on a 1988) baseline. They are now at 83 percent.

Overdelivering on Clean Water Promises

Keep in mind that these are figures for the deliberate use of mercury, not emissions per se. U.S. mercury emissions decreased approximately 45 percent between 1990 and 1999, according to the annual report. Significant reductions in emissions from municipal-waste combustors and medical-waste incinerators, by 1999, resulted from regulatory mandates under the Clean Air Act Amendments of 1990. The good news is that the U.S. has yet to see the new reductions

to be achieved from regulation of the power industry pursuant to the new Clean Air Mercury Rule which will eventually cut those mercury emissions by nearly 70 percent.

The 2004 report recognizes tremendous progress by the U.S. and Canada in reducing emissions of dioxins and furans. The U.S. projects a 92-percent reduction in nationwide releases of these pollutants by the end of 2004 against a goal of 75 percent by 2006. Nothing like under promising and over delivering! Canada stands at 84 percent and expects to meet its 2000 target of 90 percent by 2005. Again, past regulation of combustion sources has yielded these substantial reductions. When pending regulatory actions are fully implemented, "the largest source in the United States will be household garbage burning," according to the report.

This water treatment plant in New Ulm, Minnesota, helps to remove phosphorous and other pollutants from waste water before releasing it into the Minnesota River.

A Greener World than You Know

Think about it: We have done such a great job controlling dioxin emissions from large, industrial sources that we only have backyard burn barrels to go after. Check out www. openburning.org.

PCBs, second only to mercury as a cause of fish-consumption advisories nationally, is also a top priority of the Binational Toxics Strategy. The goal for high-level PCBs was a 90-percent reduction of use in electrical equipment along with proper management and disposal to prevent accidental releases. PCBs were banned by law many years ago, but they were still in use at the time the strategy was conceived. In the U.S. about 87,000 PCB transformers and 143,000 PCB capacitors were disposed of between the 1994 baseline and the end of 2002. This represents reductions of 43.5 percent and 10 percent respectively.

The 2004 Annual Progress Report on the Great Lakes Binational Toxics Strategy is a treasure trove of statistics, graphs, and general information on our sustained, continuing efforts to protect human health and the environment. Executive summary: It's a greener world than you know.

Analyze the Essay:

1. Consider what you know about G. Tracy Mehan III. What about his background makes him qualified to write an essay on water pollution? Given his credentials, are you inclined to agree or disagree with him about whether or not water pollution is a serious problem? Explain your answer.

2. G. Tracy Mehan III and the authors of the previous viewpoint, Alex Markels and Randy Dotinga, disagree over whether water pollution is a serious problem. After reading each essay, with whom do you agree? Or, is it impossible to say from these two selections? Cite evidence from the texts in your answer.

Mercury Pollution Is a Serious Problem

David Fink

In the following viewpoint, author David Fink argues that mercury pollution is a serious problem. He explains that mercury pollution from coal-fired power plants has seeped into the air and water, and is consequently found in sources of food such as fish. Exposure to mercury pollution carries many health risks, says Fink, including hindering brain development, particularly in children. The government should be doing all it can to limit mercury pollution, but according to Fink, it continues to relax regulations on mercury emissions. Fink concludes it is immoral to choose the health of industry over the health of people, and urges individual states to adopt strict measures against mercury pollution before the problem gets worse.

David Fink is a writer who lives in Connecticut. His articles have appeared in such publications as *National Wildlife* magazine, from which this viewpoint is taken.

Consider the Following Questions:

1. How many states have issued mercury warnings for fish in all of their inland water sources, as reported by the author?
2. What power source is most responsible for mercury pollution, according to the author?
3. How many newborns suffer health risks from mercury exposure each year, as reported by the author?

David Fink, "Your Health: Making Mercury Matters Worse," *National Wildlife Magazine*, vol. 42, April–May, 2004. Copyright © 2004 National Wildlife Federation. Reproduced by permission.

At what point should protecting human health take precedence over protecting an industry's bottom line? The question has come up repeatedly since Congress passed the Clean Air Act in 1970, but it took on new significance late last year [2003] when the [President George W.] Bush administration announced plans to relax federal controls on mercury emissions from power plants. The announcement caught many health professionals by surprise.

Exposure to Mercury Has Serious Health Risks

"This is a bad decision," says Dr. Philippe Grandjean, an environmental health expert at Harvard University's School of Public Health. "Mercury affects brain development and the more mercury we're exposed to, the worse off we are." Any decision that delays or stops or minimizes our abatement of mercury, he notes, will have a serious public health effect. Adds internist Dr. Judith Stein, former cochairperson of the Greater Boston Physicians for Social Responsibility: "We know without doubt that mercury poses a threat, particularly to children. This regulation will only make things worse."

Last December [2003], new Environmental Protection Agency (EPA) Administrator Michael O. Leavitt proposed that coal-fired plant operators be allowed to postpone for as long as a decade a requirement that they install modern technology to reduce mercury pollution. The

A Moral Duty to Prevent Mercury Pollution

Do we allow this . . . toxic mercury—a substance so harmful that it causes birth defects, IQ loss and mental retardation—[to] continue to poison children and pregnant women? Do we simply ignore the proliferation of warnings that fish caught in streams and lakes and rivers are unsafe to eat? . . . Or do we uphold the bipartisan work that produced the Clean Air Act, protect the health of pregnant women and children, and begin now to clean up the toxic mercury emissions?

Statement of Senator Patrick Leahy (D-VT) on S.J. Res. 20, a Resolution to Disapprove the Administration's Mercury Rule, September 13, 2005.

Coal-burning power plants like this facility in Shamokin Dam, Pennsylvania, are a major source of mercury pollution in the atmosphere.

proposal, still under review at this writing, will allow utilities to meet less stringent mercury standards as a by-product of reducing other emissions, rather than by adding new equipment. A utility could opt out of reducing mercury emissions by buying "credits" from other power facilities to meet an overall weak industry target.

Ironically, the administration's proposal was announced only days after the Food and Drug Administration issued revised warnings to women of childbearing age and young children to strictly limit their weekly consumption of fish because of concerns about mercury. The new draft advisory expanded the warnings include tuna, but it was not as strict as the advice issued by 11 states.

Mercury Pollution in Our Air, Water, and Food

The public can be exposed to mercury by everything from old thermometers to dental fillings. But coal-fired power plants remain the only unregulated—and the largest—sources of mercury pollution. Two years ago, EPA officials stated that by following current Clean Air Act requirements, power plants could feasibly cut mercury emissions by about 90 percent by 2010. Yet the Bush administration plan would reduce those emissions by only about 30 percent, even though the EPA has acknowledged the huge health risk involved.

According to the EPA, mercury has polluted 10.2 million acres of U.S. lakes, estuaries and wetlands, and 415,000 miles of streams, rivers and coasts. As a result, more than 40 states and U.S. territories have warned residents to limit consumption of certain fish, and 17 states have issued mercury advisories for fish in every inland water body.

States Must Act on Their Own

The administration's draft rule comes as seven states in the East and Midwest have adopted or are considering their own strict mercury emissions limits. The organization of New England Governors and Eastern Canadian Premiers has committed to cutting mercury levels from power plants

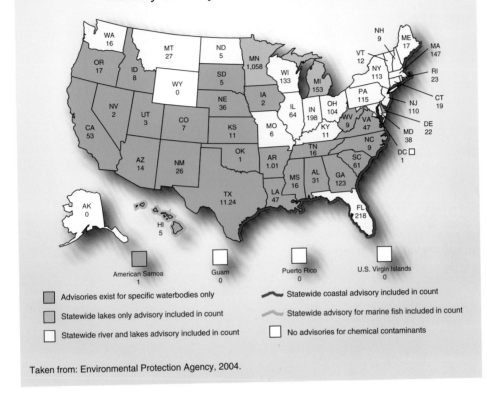

Total Number of Fish Consumption Advisories–2004

2004 Total = 3,221

The majority of U.S. states have some kind of mercury advisory alert for fish in their waters.

WA 16
MT 27
ND 5
MN 1,058
NH 9
ME 17
MA 147
OR 17
ID 8
WY 0
SD 5
WI 133
VT 12
NY 113
RI 23
NV 2
UT 3
CO 7
NE 36
IA 2
MI 153
PA 115
NJ 110
CT 19
CA 53
KS 11
MO 6
IL 64
IN 198
OH 104
WV 9
VA 47
MD 38
DE 22
AZ 14
NM 26
OK 1
AR 1.01
KY 11
TN 16
NC 9
DC □ 1
TX 11.24
LA 47
MS 16
AL 31
GA 123
SC 61
AK 0
HI 5
FL 218

American Samoa 1
Guam 0
Puerto Rico 0
U.S. Virgin Islands 0

- Advisories exist for specific waterbodies only
- Statewide lakes only advisory included in count
- Statewide river and lakes advisory included in count
- ∿ Statewide coastal advisory included in count
- ∿ Statewide advisory for marine fish included in count
- No advisories for chemical contaminants

Taken from: Environmental Protection Agency, 2004.

by 75 percent by 2010. And last year, Connecticut passed what may be the most stringent state statute, requiring a 90 percent reduction by 2008.

PSEG Power in New Jersey negotiated and agreed to the Connecticut statute for its coal-fired plant in Bridgeport. "We think there are technologies available at a reasonable cost that can deliver the kind of reductions in the Connecticut statute," says company spokesperson Neil Brown.

A Widespread Threat

Meanwhile, conservationists are concerned too few Americans are aware of the risk mercury poses. Based on

Waste from the New Almaden Quicksilver mine—which closed in 1976—litters a hillside near San Jose, California, in 2002. Quicksilver is another name for mercury, and this former mine is one of the largest sources of mercury pollution in the San Francisco Bay.

data collected by the Centers for Disease Control in 1999–2000, EPA estimates that one out of six women of childbearing age has mercury levels in her blood above the EPA's safe threshold. As a result, more than 600,000 newborns each year are at risk because of mercury exposure in the womb.

"In general women are most at risk and they are not getting adequate advice from their healthcare providers," says Felice Stadler, national policy coordinator of NWF's [National Wildlife Federation's] Clean the Rain Campaign. She points out that the mercury threat is dangerously similar to the nation's experience with lead: Each new study indicated a greater danger until, ultimately, no level was found to be safe.

"In the past," says Stadler, "we thought mercury posed a threat to only a small segment of the population, such as subsistence fishermen and sportsmen who ate a lot of fish. Now we know it's much more widespread. We should be expanding mercury controls on emissions, not relaxing them."

Analyze the Essay:

1. Examine the people that David Fink chose to quote in his essay. Make a list of each person who was quoted, and list their qualifications. What is your assessment of his sources? Does their inclusion affect your opinion of his argument? If so, in what way?

2. David Fink argues it is the government's job to protect the health of people over the health of industry. What do you think? Should the government have to choose between industry or public health? What are some ways in which compromises can be made? Explain your answer using examples from the texts you have read.

Mercury Pollution Is Not a Serious Problem

Robert Rio

In the following viewpoint, author Robert Rio argues that threats from mercury pollution have been exaggerated. He investigates an often-heard claim that a gram of mercury can pollute a 20-acre lake, but finds no credible origin for its source. He also presents a study that compares American women with Seychelles women (who eat more mercury-contaminated fish than Americans). The study found that Seychelles women's health did not suffer from eating elevated levels of mercury, causing Rio to conclude that mercury consumption does not pose a significant health risk. Rio concludes that government officials must be more responsible with the information they put out about the threat from mercury pollution.

Robert Rio is vice president of environmental programs at Associated Industries of Massachusetts.

Consider the Following Questions:

1. What is the source of the Environmental Protection Agency's claim that a gram of mercury can contaminate a 20-acre lake, according to the author?
2. What accounts for 25–30 percent of all mercury, as reported by the author?
3. For how long did scientists study 776 mother-child pairs to determine whether mercury poses a health risk?

Robert Rio, "Mercury: Grain of Truth, Gram of Nonsense," *Environment News*, March 2004. Reproduced by permission.

You have probably heard or read the oft-repeated statement, "One gram of mercury can contaminate an entire 20-acre lake." It shows up in the environmental advocates' literature as well as in EPA [Environmental Protection Agency] and state agency documents and various fact sheets on mercury. The statement is meant to scare us into believing that mishandling a thermometer or emitting even one gram of mercury would have irreversible negative consequences. And you won't be able to eat the fish, either.

All Fear, No Facts

The statement is so definitive and exact there must be scientific proof behind it, right? One gram? A 20-acre lake? Government agencies wouldn't use a statement like that unless they had actually performed the study or found one that was peer-reviewed, would they? Especially since major policy decisions are being based on it.

Clancy, a dog trained to detect traces of mercury, investigates a science classroom at North High School in Minnesota.

"One gram of mercury has the ability to contaminate a 20 acre lake," says a document on EPA's Region 9 pollution prevention Web site. The document does not cite the source for this claim.

On EPA's main Web site we find a 54-page "Economic Analysis of Including Mercury Containing Devices in the Universal Waste System, Notice of Proposed Rulemaking, February 15, 2002." "One gram of mercury," the document states, "can foul up to 5 million gallons of water." A different statement . . . this time, with a footnote. It referenced a November 16, 2000, article in the *Boston Globe*, a 400-word piece on mercury thermometers. The statement in fact appeared in the article, but again there was no attribution.

Variations on the Same Incorrect Theme

A Google search finds legislator Jon Cooper from New York writing in May 2001, "According to the EPA, a typical fever thermometer contains about one gram of mercury, enough to contaminate a 20-acre lake."

"One gram of mercury," according to the Toxics Action Center, "is enough to make the fish in a 20-acre lake unsafe to eat for a year."

After searching 150 documents through Google, it became evident all were variations on the same theme. Everybody quoted each other; no one offered attribution to anything other than press releases or generic public information documents.

They are all serious misrepresentations of the dangers of mercury, and all try to simplify what is in reality a complicated process.

Contamination Calculation

Scientists know contamination is a function of volume, not surface area. A 20-acre lake would have a surface area of 871,600 square feet. Assume an average depth of 30 feet.

That would give us 26,148,000 cubic feet—almost 200 million gallons of water. Can one gram of elemental mercury really contaminate 200 million gallons of water?

Turns out I wasn't the only one skeptical of this claim. In a letter to *Junkscience* magazine dated February 23, 2001, Dr. Kevin Wallace also cast aspersions on those claims. Wallace is director of the Occupational & Environmental Toxicology Clinic at Good Samaritan Regional Medical Center in Phoenix, Arizona. He led me to a scientist at the Minnesota Pollution Control Agency.

In Danbury, Conn., scientists have planted cottonwood trees specially designed to draw mercury out of the soil, which was contaminated here decades ago.

Ed Swain, Ph.D., of the Minnesota Pollution Control Agency, in an effort to determine the rate of atmospheric deposition of mercury in Minnesota, performed a series of core samples on several remote lakes in the state. The article he wrote, "Increasing Rate of Atmospheric Mercury Deposition in Midcontinental North America," appeared in the August 7, 1992 issue of *Science* magazine.

Based on the mercury in the core samples, he determined that in Minnesota the rate of atmospheric deposition (from rain, primarily) of mercury to a 20-acre parcel (lakes in this case) is approximately one gram per year. Swain then calculated that based on the size of Minnesota, approximately 6,000 pounds of mercury are deposited in a one-year period throughout Minnesota in order to reach the one-gram-per-20-acre conclusion. That's the data.

Nowhere does he make the conclusion that one gram of elemental mercury (like that from a thermometer) can contaminate a 20-acre lake. In fact, the study had nothing to do with the effects of mercury on water or fish.

Misunderstanding the Mercury Threat

Not only did the advocates misunderstand the study completely, but in their haste to grab headlines, they glossed over a few points in Swain's report:

- mercury deposited from natural sources (i.e., volcanic activity, ore leachate) accounts for 25–30 percent of all mercury;
- mercury deposition is a global problem;

We Needn't Worry About Mercury in Fish

How tiny are the traces of mercury in fish? University of Rochester scientists report in the *New England Journal of Medicine* that there haven't been any clinical reports of fish-related mercury poisoning since the 1950s and 1960s. . . . Environmental groups have generally kept the public in the dark about the safety cushions included in mercury advisory levels. Food scares, after all, make for good fund raising and sensational newspaper headlines.

David Martosko, "Mercury Risk? Scares Mislead American Consumers," *Milwaukee Journal-Sentinel,* August 12, 2006.

- it is the soluble form of mercury found in rain that is the problem (not the elemental form found in thermometers). Soluble mercury, through a complex transformation, goes up into the atmosphere and comes down in rain, converting to a form known as methylmercury that is absorbed by fish. Not all mercury converts to methylmercury—only about 5 percent, according to Swain, and even that is subject to some variability. And its effect on fish would be further conjecture, since that would depend on types of fish, reproduction rates, etc. In other words, it's a guess. Elemental mercury is rarely introduced to water bodies, despite the activists' thermometer analogy.

Swain's study has been misinterpreted and misquoted so many times he actually released a clarification of the study in October 2002.

Mercury in Fish Poses Very Little Risk

In the May 17, 2003 edition of *The Lancet,* one of the most respected medical journals in the world, Dr. Gary J. Myers and others from the University of Rochester Medical Center in New York present the findings of their study of mercury exposure in 776 mother-child pairs in the Seychelles islands (in the Indian Ocean) for 14 years.

The level of mercury in the ocean fish in the Seychelles is nearly identical to that in the United States (remember, mercury is a global problem). However, the women there eat fish up to 12 times per week, far more than we do in the U.S. Consequently, concentrations of mercury in indicator hair samples are many times higher among Seychelles women and their children than in the U.S.

Myers' conclusion (verbatim): "These data do not support the hypothesis that there is a neurodevelopmental risk from prenatal MeHg [methylmercury] exposure resulting solely from ocean fish consumption."

An Obligation to Tell the Truth

To my knowledge, EPA has never mentioned the results of this study in any of its literature. The May 17 report is the fifth follow-up Myers has published (others were published when the children were six months, 19 months, 29 months, and 66 months old).

We might not expect environmental advocates to have read and understood the work by Swain or Myers—but scientists at EPA and state agencies should have, and they have an obligation to present a balanced picture.

Analyze the Essay:

1. To make his argument, Robert Rio investigates the origin of sources that claim mercury pollution to be a threat. What is your opinion of this method? Is this a good way to argue against an opponent? Explain why or why not.

2. Considering what you have read in this chapter, do you believe pollution is a serious problem or an exaggerated problem? Cite evidence from at least three viewpoints in this chapter to make your argument.

Section Two:
Model Essays
and Writing
Exercises

The Five-Paragraph Essay

An *essay* is a short piece of writing that discusses or analyzes one topic. The five-paragraph essay is a form commonly used in school assignments and tests. Every five-paragraph essay begins with an *introduction,* ends with a *conclusion,* and features three *supporting paragraphs* in the middle.

The Thesis Statement. The introduction includes the essay's thesis statement. The thesis statement presents the argument or point the author is trying to make about the topic. The essays in this book all have different thesis statements because they are making different arguments about pollution.

The thesis statement should clearly tell the reader what the essay will be about. A focused thesis statement helps determine what will be in the essay; the subsequent paragraphs are spent developing and supporting its argument.

The Introduction. In addition to presenting the thesis statement, a well-written introductory paragraph captures the attention of the reader and explains why the topic being explored is important. It may provide the reader with background information on the subject matter or feature an anecdote that illustrates a point relevant to the topic. It could also present startling information that clarifies the point of the essay or put forth a contradictory position that the essay will refute. Further techniques for writing an introduction are found later in this section.

The Supporting Paragraphs. The introduction is then followed by three (or more) supporting paragraphs. These are the main body of the essay. Each paragraph presents and develops a subtopic that supports the essay's thesis statement. Each subtopic is spearheaded by a topic sentence and supported by its own facts, details, and examples. The writer can use various kinds of supporting material and details to back up the topic of each supporting paragraph. These may include statistics, quotations from people with special knowledge or expertise, historic facts, or anecdotes. A rule of writing is that specific and concrete examples are more convincing than vague, general, or unsupported assertions.

The Conclusion. The conclusion is the paragraph that closes the essay. Its function is to summarize or reiterate the main idea of the essay. It may recall an idea from the introduction or briefly examine the larger implications of the thesis. Because the conclusion is also the last chance a writer has to make an impression on the reader, it is important that it not simply repeat what has been presented elsewhere in the essay but close it in a clear, final, and memorable way.

Although the order of the essay's component paragraphs is important, they do not have to be written in the order presented here. Some writers like to decide on a thesis and write the introduction paragraph first. Other writers like to focus first on the body of the essay, and write the introduction and conclusion later.

Pitfalls to Avoid

When writing essays about controversial issues such as pollution, it is important to remember that disputes over the material are common precisely because there are many different perspectives. Remember to state your arguments in careful and measured terms. Evaluate your topic fairly—avoid overstating negative qualities of one perspective or understating positive qualities of another. Use examples, facts, and details to support any assertions you make.

The Descriptive Essay

The previous section of this book provided you with samples of published persuasive writing on pollution. Many of these essays used description to convey their message. In this section, you will focus on developing your own descriptive writing skills.

A descriptive essay gives a reader a mental picture of the subject that the writer is exploring. Typically, descriptive writing uses the five senses—sight, sound, touch, taste, and smell—to help the reader experience what the writer has experienced. A descriptive writer carefully selects vivid examples and specific details to reveal people, places, processes, events, and ideas.

Using the Descriptive Essay

While an essay can be purely descriptive, descriptive papers written for the classroom are often persuasive or expository essays that use description to make a point. Writers may also rely on description as they explain a memory or discuss an experience. For example, in Viewpoint 3, Alex Markels and Randy Dotinga describe the "cloudless sky, the blue ocean, and the soft sands" along a California beach that had been contaminated by pollution. Going into detail about the beach's beautiful qualities helps drive home the authors' point that water pollution is a serious and sad problem.

Sometimes, descriptive essays are written in the first person (from the "I" point of view). In these cases, there is no one sentence that can be singled out as the thesis statement. Instead, the essay has an *implied* thesis—a point of view made evident through the writer's careful use of details and examples.

Descriptive Writing Techniques

An important element of descriptive writing is the use of images and specific and concrete details. Specific and concrete is the opposite of general and abstract. Descriptive writers should give their readers a fuller understanding of the topic by focusing on tangible details and by appealing to the five senses. See the accompanying box for examples of general nouns and their more specific variations.

The use of *metaphors* and *similes* can also enliven descriptive writing. A *metaphor* is a word or phrase that compares two objects that are dissimilar. A simile is a metaphor that

General and Specific Descriptions

General	More specific	Most specific
vegetation	trees	fir
animal	fish	salmon
grocery item	breakfast food	cereal
sound	crash	broken glass
emotion	happiness	elation

includes the prepositions *like* or *as*. In Model Essay One, the author ends Paragraph 3 with a simile to drive home the point that swimming in a polluted body of water can be very dangerous, and even cause death.

Some descriptive essays make use of *scene* and *exposition*. The *scene* is an element commonly found in fiction and in creative writing. With scene, a writer describes an event with moment-by-moment detail, often including dialogue if people are involved. With *exposition,* a writer explains, summarizes, or concisely recounts events that occur between scenes. Scene is comparable to "showing," while exposition is similar to "telling."

Tips to Remember

A descriptive essay should give the reader a clear impression of its subject. So, a writer must select the most relevant details. A few well-chosen details are more effective than dozens of random ones. You want the reader to visualize what you are describing but not feel overloaded with information. The room you are sitting in now, for example, is likely full of many concrete and specific items. To describe the room in writing, however, you would want to choose just a few of the most vivid details that would help convey your impression of and attitude about it.

A writer should also be aware of the kinds of words he or she uses in descriptive passages. Modifying words like adjectives and adverbs can enhance descriptive writing, but they should be used sparingly. Generally, verbs and nouns are more powerful than adjectives and adverbs. The overuse of modifying words makes the writing seem "wordy" and unnatural. Compare the phrases in the accompanying box to see the difference between wordy and concise language.

In the following section, you will read some model descriptive essays about pollution and work on exercises that will help you write your own.

Wordy vs. Concise Language

Wordy	Concise
bright green potted plant with thin leaves	fern
rolling around rapidly in brilliant untamed magnificence	dancing in wild splendor
she stopped extremely abruptly	she stopped
the best most amazingly wonderful experience	fantastic time

Pollution: It's Making Us Sick

Editor's Notes The first model essay examines health problems caused by different types of pollution. The author warns that pollution is in the air, water, and food supply and uses descriptive techniques to impart the severity of the issue to the reader. The essay is structured as a five-paragraph essay wherein each paragraph focuses on a distinct, but related, pollution problem.

The notes in the margin point out key features of the essay, and will help you understand how the essay is organized. Also note that all sources are cites using MLA style. For more information on how to cite sources, see Appendix C.* As you read, consider the following:

- How does the introduction engage the reader's attention?
- What descriptive techniques are used in the essay?
- What purpose do the essay's quotes serve?
- Does the essay convince you of its point?

■ Refers to thesis and topic sentences

■ Refers to supporting details

Paragraph 1

Except for explicit instances of trash in their yard or acid rain ruining the paint job on their car, people rarely pay close attention to the personal toll pollution takes on their lives. This is because often we cannot see, smell, or taste the pollution that is most dangerous to us. But be forewarned: Pollution is in the air, the water, and the food supply and is slowly poisoning us all.

This is the essay's thesis statement. It previews the topics that will be discussed.

* In applying MLA style guidelines in this book, thefollowing simplifications have been made: Parenthetical text citationsare confined to direct quotations only; electronic sourcedocumentation in the works cited list omits date of access, pageranges, and some detailed facts of publication.

Paragraph 2

The author sets the scene by allowing the reader to envision two polluted environments. Did you find this effective?

Climb a tall hill in Los Angeles and note the dingy film that hangs in the air over the city. That's smog, some of the worst in the country. Smog exists in most major cities; stand on a street corner in mid-town Manhattan, for example, and take a deep breath. You are likely to catch a big whiff of fine particle pollution, the soot, dirt, and toxins that make up air pollution. Your eyes might water; your throat may tickle. Beyond these symptoms, fine particle pollution can cause dozens of diseases. Air pollution causes serious cardiovascular problems, including asthma, heart attacks, strokes, lung cancer, even death. According to Clean Air advocate Supryia Ray, fine particles emitted from U.S. power plants cause 23,600 premature deaths, 38,200 nonfatal heart attacks, and 554,000 asthma attacks every year. In fact, the "Environmental Protection Agency (EPA) has estimated that particle pollution shortens the lives of its victims by an average of 14 years" (Ray, 7).

This quote is taken from Viewpoint 1. Note how the author has taken care to give the author of the viewpoint credit and quote her words exactly.

Paragraph 3

This sentence smoothly transitions from the previous idea, and provides the topic sentence for paragraph 3.

Americans aren't only getting sick from the air they breathe—even going for a swim at a public beach can be a hazardous, even deadly, experience. In 2003, American beaches collectively had more than 18,000 unhealthy days. On these days, thousands of beaches on America's shoreline posted advisories that warned people against getting in the water for fear of contracting dangerous bacteria. These insidious microorganisms cause a wide range of illnesses, including gastrointestinal illnesses, rashes, and viruses. One surfer in Malibu, California, even died after contracting a viral disease called myocarditis, which caused his heart to swell to the point it killed him! These beaches are polluted by outdated sewer systems, overrun septic systems, pesticide runoff, even fecal matter. It turns out that taking a casual summer swim at the wrong beach is as dangerous as gulping a bottle of poison.

Always use specific examples. The more clearly your reader can picture your subject, the better.

The author uses a simile to make more powerful the consequences of swimming at a polluted beach.

Paragraph 4

If you survived a walk through a city and a day at a beach, don't relax yet: You could still get sick from your dinner. In addition to the pesticides embedded in nonorganic produce, that tuna melt you ordered could be chock full of mercury. Indeed, "mercury has polluted 10.2 million acres of U.S. lakes, estuaries and wetlands, and 415,000 miles of streams, rivers and coasts. As a result, more than 40 states and U.S. territories have warned residents to limit consumption of certain fish, and 17 states have issued mercury advisories for fish in every inland water body" (Fink). Ingesting high levels of mercury can cause health damage, especially to children and the unborn. Mercury seeps slowly into the womb, hampering brain development. Pregnant women must especially be careful, then, that their fish dinners do not come with mercury and mashed potatoes on the side.

> This quote was taken from Viewpoint 5. Learn how to retain information that may be used to support points you make in your essays.

> These are good examples of descriptive details. They make the essay more interesting and unique.

Paragraph 5

From the air to the water to the dinner table, pollution has become a problem that has enormous consequences for human health. The next time you take a deep breath, imagine your pink, fleshy lungs slowly eroding from breathing soot and dust. The next time you swim in the ocean, try to picture the warm sea of bacteria and fecal matter floating all around you. Then let these images propel you to take action against pollution in our communities. It is not until people realize the great toll pollution takes on our health that they will become active in trying to reduce it.

> This is the topic sentence of paragraph 5. It completes the essay without repeating what has already been stated.

> Note how the author has used graphic, vivid details to reinforce her argument.

Works Cited

Supryia Ray, "Plagued by Pollution: Unsafe Levels of Soot Pollution in 2005." U.S. Public Interest Research Group (U.S. PIRG) Education Fund Jan. 2006: 1–28.

David Fink, "Your Health: Making Mercury Matters Worse," *National Wildlife* 42, no. 3 (April–May 2004).

Exercise 1A: Create an Outline from an Existing Essay

It often helps to create an outline of the five-paragraph essay before you write it. The outline can help you organize the information, arguments, and evidence you have gathered with your research. For this exercise, create an outline that could have been used to write "Pollution: It's Making Us Sick." This "reverse engineering" exercise is meant to help familiarize you with how outlines can help classify and arrange information.

To do this you will need to
1. articulate the essay's thesis,
2. pinpoint important pieces of evidence,
3. flag quotes that supported the essay's ideas, and
4. identify key points that supported the argument.

Part of the outline has already been started to give you an idea of the assignment.

Outline

I. Paragraph One

    A. Write the essay's thesis:

II. Paragraph Two

Topic: For this exercise, create an outline that could have been used to write *Pollution: It's Making You Sick*. Identify topic sentences and provide at least two supporting details for each sentence. This "reverse engineering" exercise is meant to help familiarize you with how outlines can help classify and arrange information.

A.

B.

III. Paragraph Three

Topic:

A. Dangerous microorganisms found in polluted water cause a wide range of illnesses, including gastrointestinal illnesses, rashes, and viruses.

B.

IV. Paragraph Four

Topic:

A. Quote from David Fink: "mercury has polluted 10.2 million acres of U.S. lakes, estuaries and wetlands, and 415,000 miles of streams, rivers and coasts. As a result, more than 40 states and U.S. territories have warned residents to limit consumption of certain fish, and 17 states have issued mercury advisories for fish in every inland water body."

B.

V. Paragraph Five

A. Write the essay's conclusion:

Exercise 1B: Using Quotations to Enliven Your Essay

Quotations are an important part of every essay, and especially descriptive essays. Get in the habit of using quotes to support at least some of the ideas in your essays. Quotes do not need to appear in every paragraph, but often enough so that the essay contains voices aside from your own. When you write, use quotations to accomplish the following:

- Provide expert advice that you are not necessarily in the position to know about.
- Cite lively or passionate passages.
- Include a particularly well-written point that gets to the heart of the matter.
- Supply statistics or facts that have been derived from someone's research.
- Deliver anecdotes that illustrate the point you are trying to make.
- Express first-person testimony.

There are a couple of important things to remember when using quotations.

- Note your sources' qualifications and biases. This way your reader can identify the person you have quoted and can put their words in context.
- Put any quoted material within proper quotation marks. Failing to attribute quotes to their authors constitutes plagiarism, which is when an author takes someone else's words or ideas and presents them as their own. Plagiarism is a very serious infraction and must be avoided at all costs.

Problem One: Reread the essays presented in all sections of this book and find at least one example of each of the above quotation types.

Every essay features introductory and concluding paragraphs that are used to frame the main ideas being presented. Along with presenting the essay's thesis statement, well-written introductions should grab the attention of the reader and make clear why the topic being explored is important. The conclusion reiterates the essay's thesis and is also the last chance for the writer to make an impression on the reader. Strong introductions and conclusions can greatly enhance an essay's effect on an audience.

The Introduction

There are several techniques that can be used to craft an introductory paragraph. An essay can start with:

- an anecdote: a brief story that illustrates a point relevant to the topic;
- startling information: facts or statistics that elucidate the point of the essay;
- setting up and knocking down a position: a position or claim believed by proponents of one side of a controversy, followed by statements that challenge that claim;
- historical perspective: an example of the way things used to be that leads into a discussion of how or why things work differently now;
- summary information: general introductory information about the topic that feeds into the essay's thesis statement.

Problem One

Reread the introductory paragraphs of the model essays and of the viewpoints in Section I. Identify which of the techniques described above are used in the example essays. How do they grab the attention of the reader? Are their thesis statements clearly presented?

Paragraph 2

What descriptive details are found in paragraph 2? What specific information is provided?

First, students partnered themselves with local organizations that already coordinated beach cleanups. The students helped promote the beach cleanups by designing and printing flyers, stickers, and posters. They even created a Web site where students and other members of the community could find out about cleanup events and sign up to attend. After selecting a date and a beach to clean, the students showed up early to get organized. They created a welcome counter at which volunteers could sign up and get cleanup supplies such as rubber gloves, trash bags, and trash pickup tools. They thought of ways to generate excitement about the beach cleanup; for example, they sponsored a contest in which whoever took the most trash off the beach that day would get a prize.

Paragraph 3

This is paragraph 3's topic sentence. Note how it broadly states what will be covered in the paragraph.

When students finally got out on the beach and dug around in the sand, they were appalled by what they found. They picked up thousands of cigarette butts; bits of plastic; foam; mangled toys; old soda cans; food wrappers; and other trash and debris that had been either left onshore or had washed up on it. "The most disturbing thing we found was needles and drug paraphernalia," said Padron. "If you stretch your arm out in the sand or something that's really dangerous. It's disturbing that people leave that there." Over the course of the two-hour beach cleanup, Padron and ten other students cleaned more than four acres of beach and carted away more than 210 pounds of trash!

Paragraph 4

Padron's comments lend the essay a personal feel. Make sure to integrate unique and interesting quotes from those you interview in your essays.

After finishing the beach cleanup, the High Tech High students were invigorated. "It was such a cool thing to be part of, and we could really see the difference we made in the beach," said Padron. She encourages students from around the country to participate in cleanups wherever they are needed; on beaches, lakefronts, parks, even around their schools. "Don't be afraid," says Padron, "you don't have to organize a huge thing. Just try and see the need in your neighborhood. If you see wrappers, pick 'em up, throw 'em away. It'll make you feel good."

Paragraph 5

Community service projects such as beach cleanups go a long way toward both helping the environment and getting people involved in their communities. There is plenty of reward for taking part in these types of charitable communities. Said Padron of her experience organizing the beach cleanup: "It's a really good feeling—to go out and give a little to your community, knowing you made your town safer and cleaner: You get a sense of pride in that." For more information on beach cleanups and to get ideas on how to organize your own cleanup, visit www.beachcleanups.org.

When writing an essay, it is a good idea to conclude by letting your readers know where they can find more information on the event or subject.

Works Cited

Bianca Padron interviewed by Lauri S. Friedman, 7 Jun. 2007."

Exercise 2A: Conducting an Interview

Model essay two, *A Day at the Beach Cleanup*, was written after conducting an interview with seventeen-year-old Bianca Padron, who organized the cleanup. When reporting on events that occur in your community, you will probably need to interview people to get critical information and opinions. Interviews allow you to get the story behind a participant's experiences, enabling you to provide a fuller picture of the event.

The key to a successful interview is asking the right questions. You want the respondent to answer in as much detail as possible so you can write an accurate, colorful, and interesting piece. Therefore, you should have a clear idea of what general pieces of information you want to find out from the respondent before you begin interviewing. The five classic journalist questions—who, what, when, where, why, and how—are an excellent place to begin. If you get answers to each of these questions, you will end up with a pretty good picture of the event.

There are many ways to conduct an interview, but the following suggestions will help you get started:

Step I: Choose a setting with little distraction.

Avoid bright lights or loud noises, and make sure the person you are interviewing feels comfortable speaking to you. Professional settings such as offices and places of business are always appropriate settings for an interview. If it is a phone interview, be sure you can clearly hear what the person is saying (so do not conduct the interview on a cell phone while walking on a busy city block, for example).

Step II: Explain who you are and what you intend to learn from the interview.

Identify yourself. For what publication are you writing? If you are writing for a school paper, identify the paper. If you are conducting research for an ongoing project, explain the project's goals and in what way you expect the interviewee can help you reach them. Indicate how long you expect the interview to take, and get all contact information upfront.

Step III: Ask specific questions and start at the beginning.

Make sure you ask at least two questions that address each of the following ideas: who, what, where, when, why, and how. Who was involved in the event? What happened during the course of the event? Where did it take place? Specific questions will change depending on what type of event you are covering. Follow your instincts; if you don't know something or have a question, ask. The answer will likely yield good information that will enhance your essay.

Step IV: Take notes.

Never rely on your memory when conducting an interview. Either type or jot down notes, or ask permission to tape or otherwise record the interview.

Step V: Verify quotes and information.

Before you write your report, it is important to go back to your source to double check key points of information. Also, you must run any quotes you intend to use by the source before you put them in your essay. This is to make sure you heard the person accurately and are not misrepresenting their position.

Types of Questions to Ask During an Interview

Questions you will ask your interviewee tend to fall in a few basic categories.

Knowledge—what they know about the topic or event. This can include historical background, logistics, and outcomes of an event. For example, Bianca Padron in Model Essay Two provided the interviewer with information about the purpose of the beach cleanups, who was involved, what was found, and how much trash was carted off the beach.

Sensory—ask questions about what people have seen, touched, heard, tasted, or smelled. These details will help your readers vividly imagine the event you are reporting on. Padron, for example, noted that the students found used needles and other drug paraphernalia at the beach cleanup. Her shock and disgust, along with her concern for the safety of beachgoers, came across in the sensory details and statements she provided to the interviewer.

Behavior—what motivated the person to become involved in this project or movement? What do they hope to gain by having their story publicized?

Opinions, values, and feelings—what the person thinks about the topic or event. These type of questions result in opinionated or personal statements that you, as an objective reporter, most likely will not make in your essay. However, you can impart the emotion behind an event—such as pride, sadness, anger, or excitement—through the opinionated and emotional quotes you collect.

Exercise 2B: Report on an Event

Reports show up in many publications—newspapers, magazines, journals, Web logs (blogs) are just some of the places people turn to read about events and activities underway in their community.

Think about the type of event you'd like to report on. It could be a trip summary; the happenings of a local event, such as a parade or cleanup; a sports game; a party; or another experience in which people are coming together to get something done. Think next about the type of publication in which your report would best appear. Trip summaries, or travelogues, make great fodder for blogs; reports on school events such as sports games or performances are best featured in the school paper.

Before you report on an event, make sure you have done thorough research. Look over all notes from your interviews. Outline a road map for your essay to follow (see exercises in this book on how to outline an essay prior to writing it). Examine where quotations, information, and other details will fit best. After you absorb and organize all the information you have collected, you are ready to write.

News reports tend to be objective, so make sure your writing style is impartial and matter-of-fact. Also, be sure to provide the reader with enough information to visualize the event, but not so much that you bombard them with unnecessary or unrelated details. Use the other writing exercises found in this book—on using quotations, writing introductions and conclusions, and gathering research—to help you write the report. Then submit it for publication!

You Can Never Go Back

Editor's Notes Essays drawn from memories or personal experiences are called personal narratives. The following essay is this type of essay. It is not based on research or the retelling of someone else's experiences, such as other descriptive essays you have read in this book. Instead, this essay consists of an autobiographical story that recounts memories of an event that happened to someone involving pollution.

The essay differs from the first two model essays in that it is written in the subjective or first-person ("I") point of view. It is also different in that it is more than five paragraphs. Many ideas require more than five paragraphs in order to be adequately developed. Moreover, the ability to write a sustained paper is a valuable skill. Learning how to develop a longer piece of writing gives you the tools you will need to advance academically. Indeed, many colleges, universities, and academic programs require candidates to submit a personal narrative as part of the application process.

As you read the following essay, take note of the sidebars in the margin. Pay attention to how the essay is organized and presented.

Refers to thesis and topic sentences

Refers to supporting details

Paragraph 1

Although less formal and more creative than other thesis statements that appear in this book, the essay starts with a thesis that establishes the general topic and direction of the essay.

In what ways is this introduction different from the other introductory paragraphs you have read in this section?

You can never go back in time. I learned this the hard way in 2007, when I tried to revisit one of my most beloved childhood places: Lake Kippacabo, a sprawling lake in northern Maine. In the summer of 1986, my family rented a cabin along the banks of Lake Kippacabo. The house was beautiful: a big, yellow home shrouded by trees. Sticking out from the house was a private dock, with two canoes, two kayaks, and a sailboat loosely floating in the water. I remember how, upon seeing the boats, my sister and I squealed with delight.

Paragraph 2

"Dad," I yelled back toward the house. "Are these boats for us?!"

"They sure are sweetheart!" His voice boomed from the inside of the cabin. "Let me help your mother unpack and then we'll take them out."

Being out in the middle of the crystal clear lake was something I'll never forget. The water was so clean that when the sun's rays came out in full force, you could see twenty feet through the water column! We fished right off the end of the boat and caught enough bass and sunfish to cook for dinner almost every night.

Make a list of the specific details used to bring this essay to life. Such details include colors, numbers, shapes, sizes, and adjectives. In what instances are these details used, and what do they add to the essay?

Paragraph 3

That summer, I practically lived in the lake. As I waited for my mom to cook breakfast, I would stand on the lakeshore, skipping rocks across the clear, placid surface. An hour later I could be found doing laps back and forth in front of the cabin, my mother keeping a watchful eye on my bright red bathing suit to make sure she could see me at all times. I often ate my lunches on the deck of the sailboat and spent the dusky evenings watching the sun slowly set from the center of the lake, where I felt like I was queen of a private aqua universe.

What similes and metaphors does the author use to enhance the essay?

Paragraph 4

The memories of that summer on Lake Kippacabo stayed with me throughout my childhood years and well into adulthood. During times of stress or sorrow, I would think back to the image of myself on a small boat in the center of a huge lake and feel calm and happy. For the occasion of my thirtieth birthday, then, I decided what I really wanted was a trip back to the lake, to where I had experienced such pure happiness and childhood delight. I called my sister, rallying her to making the long journey back in time with me.

Paragraph 5

Does the dialogue sound natural to you? What details or features enhance it?

"Karen, it's me. Listen, what do you think of taking a trip to Maine with me this summer?"

"Maine? What could you possibly want to do in Maine?" She thought about it for a minute. "I know—you want to go back to Kippacabo, don't you!"

She could almost hear me grinning through the phone. "Yes! Come on, it'll be wonderful. Two sisters returning to their stomping grounds."

"I don't know," she said. "I've got a lot of work to do. Besides," I could hear the hesitation in her voice. "That was such a great summer. Don't you kind of want to keep the memory preserved the way it is? I mean, what if it's all different?"

How is foreshadowing used in this paragraph? What purpose does it serve?

I scoffed. "Are you kidding? If anyplace was timeless, it was the banks of that lake. I bet it's exactly the same!"

Paragraph 6

Note how using particular details helps the scene come to life and build anticipation in the reader.

After some steady persuasion, my sister agreed to travel to Maine and revisit the lake with me. For months we planned the trip, shrieking in delight every time we thought about once again owning the center of the lake from a canoe or kayak. Finally, when the weekend arrived, we rented a car and drove up highway 95, passing lobster shacks and boating rental places as we headed toward the lake. We drove down the graveled road toward the house, and it was just as I remembered it! The green trees were so dense they obscured everything but the patch of road directly beneath us. I could feel my inner child getting ready to do laps in the lake and reclaim the throne of her aqua universe.

Paragraph 7

But as soon as the car turned up the driveway to the house, I could barely believe my eyes. The bright yellow cabin I remembered so well was nothing more than a dilapidated shack with a rotted porch and boarded-up windows. The dock that had once sprung from the house was also rotted, whole chunks of it missing.

Paragraph 8

But worse than the condition of the house was the condition of the lake. Instead of being greeted by the sparkling blue aquatic expanse of my childhood, I found myself gazing upon a brown, murky pit of slime and pollution. Rusted soda cans and bits of plastic clung to the shore. The water, which once I could peer twenty feet below the surface, was now so dingy and opaque it actually showed my own reflection. The lakeside reeked of sulfur and a thick scummy film encrusted much of the water surface.

> Can you picture the scene the author describes? What details allow you to visualize it best?

Paragraph 9

We later learned that in the twenty years since we had first visited, the area around Lake Kippacabo had become increasingly developed. Toxic runoff from increased commercial and residential development had slowly strangled the lake. The runoff killed much of the fish and other lake life and poisoned the trees around the lake shore. Compounding the problem was poor sewage systems not equipped to handle the increased population. Therefore, any time it rained, toxic bacteria and chemicals such as phosphorus overflowed into the lake. Eventually, the lake's systems could not clean it further—it succumbed to pollution, leaving behind a watery graveyard.

> Note how the point of the essay is implicitly, rather than explicitly, made. Sometimes it is more powerful to let actions speak for themselves rather than trying to explain the obvious.

Paragraph 10

It turns out my sister was right; the childhood images I held of Lake Kippacabo were forever tainted by the visit back to the lake. I should have known that one can never go back in time—especially to a time before pollution. I wonder: Will pollution ruin all of our natural resources, leaving us with only our memories?

> The narrative has returned to the topic established in the opening paragraph.

Exercise 3A: Practice Writing a Scene with Dialogue

The previous model essay used scene and dialogue to make a point. For this exercise, you will practice creative writing techniques to draft a one or two paragraph scene with dialogue. First, take another look at model essay three and examine how dialogue is used.

When writing dialogue, it is important to:

1. Use natural-sounding language.
2. Include a few details showing character gestures and expressions as they speak.
3. Avoid overuse of speaker tags with modifiers, such as "he said stupidly," "she muttered softly," "I shouted angrily," and so on.
4. Indent and create a new paragraph when speakers change.
5. Place quotation marks at the beginning of and at the end of a character's speech. Do not enclose each sentence of a speech in quotation marks.

But I Can't Write That

One aspect about personal descriptive writing is that you are revealing to the reader something about yourself. Many people enjoy this part of writing. Others are not so sure about sharing their personal stories—especially if they reveal something embarrassing or something that could get them in trouble. In these cases, what are your options?

- Talk with your teacher about your concerns. Will this narrative be shared in class? Can the teacher pledge confidentiality?
- Change the story from being about yourself to a story about a friend. This will involve writing in the third person rather than the first person.

- Change a few identifying details and names to disguise characters and settings.
- Pick a different topic or thesis that you do not mind sharing.

Write Your Own Descriptive Five-Paragraph Essay

Using the information in this book, write your own five-paragraph descriptive essay that deals with pollution. You can use the resources in this book for information about issues relating to this topic and how to structure this type of essay.

The following steps are suggestions on how to get started.

Step One: Choose your topic.

The first step is to decide what topic to write your descriptive essay on. Is there any subject that particularly fascinates you? Is there an issue you strongly support or feel strongly against? Is there a topic you feel personally connected to or one that you would like to learn more about? Ask yourself such questions before selecting your essay topic. Refer to Appendix D, "Sample Essay Topics," if you need help selecting a topic.

Step Two: Write down questions and answers about the topic.

Before you begin writing, you will need to think carefully about what ideas your essay will contain. This is a process known as *brainstorming*. Brainstorming involves asking yourself questions and coming up with ideas to discuss in your essay. Possible questions that will help you with the brainstorming process include:

- Why is this topic important?
- Why should people be interested in this topic?
- How can I make this essay interesting to the reader?
- What question am I going to address in this paragraph or essay?
- What facts, ideas, or quotes can I use to support the answer to my question?

Questions especially for descriptive essays include:

- Have I chosen a compelling story to examine?
- Have I used vivid details?
- Have I made scenes come alive for my reader?
- What qualities do my characters have? Are they interesting?
- Does my descriptive essay have a clear beginning, middle, and end?
- Does my essay evoke a particular emotion or response from the reader?

Step Three: Gather facts, ideas, and anecdotes related to your topic.

This book contains several places to find information, including the viewpoints and the appendixes. In addition, you may want to research the books, articles, and Web sites listed in section III or do additional research in your local library. You can also conduct interviews if you know someone who has a compelling story that would fit well in your essay.

Step Four: Develop a workable thesis statement.

Use what you have written down in steps 2 and 3 to help you articulate the main point or argument you want to make in your essay. It should be expressed in a clear sentence and make an arguable or supportable point.

Example:

Recycling programs should be mandatory in all schools, housing developments, places of business, and public institutions.

(This could be the thesis statement of a descriptive essay that argues that enforcing mandatory recycling programs can help reduce pollution.)

Step Five: Write an outline or diagram.
a. Write the thesis statement at the top of the outline.
b. Write Roman numerals I, II, and III on the left side of the page.

c. Next to each Roman numeral, write down the best ideas you came up with in step 3. These should all directly relate to and support the thesis statement.

d. Next to each letter write down information that supports that particular idea.

Step Six: Write the three supporting paragraphs.

Use your outline to write the three supporting paragraphs. Write down the main idea of each paragraph in sentence form. Do the same thing for the supporting points of information. Each sentence should support the paragraph of the topic. Be sure you have relevant and interesting details, facts, and quotes. Use transitions when you move from idea to idea to keep the text fluid and smooth. Sometimes, although not always, paragraphs can include a concluding or summary sentence that restates the paragraph's argument.

Step Seven: Write the introduction and conclusion.

See Exercise 1C for information on writing introductions and conclusions.

Step Eight: Read and rewrite.

As you read, check your essay for the following:

✔ Does the essay maintain a consistent tone?

✔ Do all paragraphs reinforce your general thesis?

✔ Do all paragraphs flow from one to the other? Do you need to add transition words or phrases?

✔ Have you quoted from reliable, authoritative, and interesting sources?

✔ Is there a sense of progression throughout the essay?

✔ Does the essay get bogged down in too much detail or irrelevant material?

✔ Does your introduction grab the reader's attention?

✔ Does your conclusion reflect back on any previously discussed material, or give the essay a sense of closure?

✔ Are there any spelling or grammatical errors?

Section Three:
Supporting
Research
Material

Facts About Pollution

Editor's Note: These facts can be used in reports to reinforce or add credibility when making important points.

Recycling

Trash can take decades, even centuries, to decompose. According to the National Parks Service, it takes a:

Glass Bottle .... 1 million years
to decompose

Fishing Line.. 600 years

Plastic Beverage Bottle .... 450 years

Disposable Diaper .... 450 years

Aluminum Can... 80–200 years

Foamed Plastic Buoy............................... 80 years

Foamed Plastic Cup .... 50 years

Rubber-Boot Sole .... 50–80 years

Tin Can .... 50 years

Leather .... 50 years

Nylon Fabric .... 30–40 years

Plastic Film Container .... 20–30 years

Plastic Bag... 10–20 years

Cigarette Butt .... 1–5 years

Wool Sock .... 1–5 years

Plywood .... 1–3 years

Waxed Milk Carton .... 3 months

Apple Core .... 2 months

Newspaper... 6 weeks

Orange or Banana Peel .... 2–5 weeks

Paper Towel... 2–4 weeks

According to the Environmental Protection Agency:

- 42 percent of the paper thrown away in the United States is recycled.
- 40 percent of plastic soft drink bottles are recycled.

- 55 percent of aluminum soft drink and beer cans are recycled.
- 57 percent of steel packaging is recycled.
- 52 percent of all major appliances are recycled.

According to the organization Health Care without Harm:

- The average American throws away six hundred times his or her adult weight in garbage every year. This adds up to more than ninety thousand pounds of garbage over a lifetime.
- With the amount of energy it takes to make one new aluminum can, twenty cans can be made from recycled aluminum.

According to beverage industry consultant R.W. Beck, Inc.:

- 40 million plastic bottles—most of them from bottled water—are thrown in the trash or tossed as litter every day.
- Only 12 percent of plastic bottles from water, juice, and sports beverages are recycled, compared with 30 percent of soft drink bottles.

According to the National Recycling Coalition, the Environmental Protection Agency, and Earth911.org:

- A used aluminum can is recycled and back on the grocery shelf as a new can in as little as sixty days.
- Used aluminum beverage cans are the most recycled item in the United States, but other types of aluminum, such as siding, gutters, car components, storm-window frames, and lawn furniture can also be recycled.
- Recycling one aluminum can saves enough energy to run a TV for three hours, which is the equivalent of a half a gallon of gasoline.
- There is no limit to the amount of times an aluminum can be recycled.

- Five hundred thousand trees must be cut down to produce each week's Sunday papers.
- Recycling a single run of the Sunday New York Times would save seventy-five thousand trees.
- The average American uses seven trees a year in paper, wood, and other products made from trees. This amounts to about 2 billion trees per year.
- The amount of wood and paper thrown away each year is enough to heat 50 million homes for twenty years.
- Americans use 85 million tons of paper a year; about 680 pounds per person.
- The average household throws away thirteen thousand separate pieces of paper each year. Most is packaging and junk mail.
- Americans use 2.5 million plastic bottles every hour.
- American throw away 25 billion Styrofoam coffee cups every year.
- The energy saved from recycling one glass bottle can run a 100-watt light bulb for four hours. It also causes 20 percent less air pollution and 50 percent less water pollution than when a new bottle is made from raw materials.

Landfills

- About one-third of an average dump is made up of packaging material.
- Every year, each American uses about twelve hundred pounds of organic garbage that can be composted to landfills.
- The highest point in Ohio is "Mount Rumpke," which is actually a mountain of trash at the Rumpke sanitary landfill!
- On average, it costs thirty dollars per ton to recycle trash, fifty dollars to send it to the landfill, and sixty-five to seventy-five dollars to incinerate it.

- According to the Competitive Enterprise Institute, it costs about five hundred dollars to recycle a ton of electronics waste but only about forty dollars to put it in a landfill.

Air Pollution

The Centers for Disease Control and Prevention estimate that together, American students miss 14 million school days and adults miss 12 million work days every year because of asthma.

According to the Foundation for Clean Air Progress:

- Since 1970, Americans have cut releases of air pollutants by more than 50 million tons.
- It would take twenty of today's new cars to generate the same amount of air pollution as one mid-1960s model car. In another ten years, thanks to new automotive and fuel technologies, it will take thirty-three cars to produce the air pollution emissions of one mid-1960s model.
- Compared with just ten years ago, America's largest cities are recording dramatically fewer days on which air pollution exceeds federal standards.
- One major air pollutant, lead, is nearly gone from the air. Since the mid-1970s, levels of airborne lead are down 96 percent.

According to the Environmental Protection Agency:

- Driving a car is the single most polluting thing that most Americans do.
- In many cities, cars and trucks are the most significant cause of ground-level ozone pollution.

According to the Sierra Club:

- Cars and light trucks account for 20 percent of the nation's annual carbon dioxide pollution.
- One gallon of gasoline burned puts twenty-eight pounds of carbon dioxide into the atmosphere.

- U.S. national parks are being degraded by poor air quality. Smog levels were measured in twenty-eight national parks from 1993 to 2002. At twenty of these national parks, smog levels increased over the ten-year period. Improvements were only seen in six parks and most of the improvements were not significant.
- **Shenandoah National Park:** On particularly bad air days, visibility at the park may drop to less than one mile.
- **Sequoia-Kings Canyon National Park:** In 2004, air in the park was unhealthy to breath on fifty-two days. Signs warned visitors against taking long hikes.
- **Yosemite National Park:** Over an eleven-year-study period, bad air levels in the park exceeded those found in many major metropolitan areas, including Atlanta, New York, and Houston.
- **Great Smoky Mountains National Park:** Scenic views at the nation's most visited national park have been reduced by 80 percent from natural conditions.

Water Pollution

In 2003, America's beaches issued more than eighteen thousand closings and warnings due to water pollution, according to the National Resources Defense Council.

According to the U.S. House of Representatives Committee on Resources:

- Less than 5 percent of water sources are poor quality or severely polluted. In 1961, 30 percent of water sources fell under those categories.
- In 2002, about 94 percent of the population that received its water from community water systems was served by systems meeting all health-based standards. Only 79 percent were served by similarly clean systems in 1993.
- Since the National Coastal Wetlands Conservation Grant Program began in 1990, over 167,000 acres of wetlands have been protected or restored.

According to the Virginia Department of Conservation and Recreation:

- The amount of water on Earth does not change, although it may appear as water, ice, or water vapor at any given time.
- There are 326 million cubic miles of water on Earth. A cubic mile contains 1 trillion gallons.
- Only 3 percent of the earth's water is freshwater. Two percent is frozen in ice caps and glaciers, leaving only about 1 percent of the earth's water available for human, plant, and animal consumption.
- Demand for freshwater by humans doubled between 1989 and 2000.
- By the year 2020, the United States will produce three times the sewage it did in 1970.
- In the southeast region of the United States, only 8 percent of the stream miles are polluted. Streams in other regions are more polluted: Pacific states 25 percent, southern plains 29 percent, northeast 40 percent, northern plains 42 percent.

According to the Environmental Protection Agency:

- The five Great Lakes—Superior, Michigan, Huron, Erie, and Ontario—hold one-fifth of the freshwater on the earth's surface, and 80 percent of the lake and river water in North America.
- Less than 1 percent of the water in the Great Lakes is replaced each year by precipitation.
- New chemicals of concern, like polybrominated diphenyl ethers used as flame retardants, and various pharmaceutical and personal care products, are being detected more frequently in the Great Lakes.
- Nonnative species (zebra mussels, spiny water fleas) continue to invade the Great Lakes and impair the food web.

- Declines in the duration and extent of ice cover on the Great Lakes and declines in lake levels due to evaporation during the winter are expected to occur in future years.
- Continuing wetlands loss and degradation results in loss of habitat for birds, amphibians, fish, and wildlife.
- Aquatic habitats on the Great Lake coasts continue to deteriorate due to development, shoreline hardening, and nonnative species.

Mercury Pollution

- Forty-five states have issued official warnings that fish in their waters contained levels of mercury high enough to threaten human health.
- The Environmental Protection Agency estimates that half of the mercury in American waterways comes from domestic pollution.
- Approximately 630,000 children are born each year at risk for brain damage because of elevated mercury level's in their blood, according to the Environmental Protection Agency.
- Mercury pollution has contaminated 10.2 million acres of American lakes, estuaries, and wetlands, and 415,000 miles of streams, rivers, and coasts, according to a 2002 estimate by the Environmental Protection Agency.
- Mercury emissions in the United States dropped by more than 42 percent from 1995 to 2006, according to the U.S. House Committee on Resources.

Finding and Using Sources of Information

No matter what type of essay you are writing, it is necessary to find information to support your point of view. You can use sources such as books, magazine articles, newspaper articles, and online articles.

Using Books and Articles

You can find books and articles in a library by using the library's computer or cataloging system. If you are not sure how to use these resources, ask a librarian to help you. You can also use a computer to find many magazine articles and other articles written specifically for the Internet.

You are likely to find a lot more information than you can possibly use in your essay, so your first task is to narrow it down to what is likely to be most usable. Look at book and article titles. Look at book chapter titles and examine the book's index to see if it contains information on the specific topic you want to write about. (For example, if you want to write about mercury pollution and you find a book about coal-fired power plants, check the chapter titles and index to be sure the book contains information relating to mercury emissions and pollution before you bother to checkout the book.)

For a five-paragraph essay, you do not need a great deal of supporting information, so quickly try to narrow down your materials to a few good books and magazine or Internet articles. You do not need dozens. You might even find that one or two good books or articles contain all the information you need.

You probably do not have time to read an entire book, so find the chapters or sections that relate to your topic and skim these. When you find useful information, copy it onto a note card or notebook. You should look for supporting facts, statistics, quotations, and examples.

Using the Internet

When you select your supporting information, it is important that you evaluate its source. This is especially important with information you find on the Internet. Because nearly anyone can put information on the Internet, there is as much bad information as good information. Before using Internet information—or any information—try to determine if the source seems to be reliable. Is the author or Internet site sponsored by a legitimate organization? Is it from a government source? Does the author have any special knowledge or training relating to the topic you are looking up? Does the article give any indication of where its information comes from?

Using Your Supporting Information

When you use supporting information from a book, article, interview, or other source, there are three important things to remember:

1. *Make it clear whether you are using a direct quotation or a paraphrase.* If you copy information directly from your source, you are quoting it. You must put quotation marks around the information, and tell where the information comes from. If you put the information in your own words, you are paraphrasing it.

Here is an example of a using a quotation:

Although asthma and air pollution are often causally linked, there is much research showing that air pollution is not the chief cause of asthma and may in fact have no bearing on increased cases in the United States. As one air pollution expert puts it, "Environmentalists and regulators depend on public fear and outrage over air pollution for their funding, jobs, and power. Claiming that air pollution causes asthma serves their needs by linking air pollution to a serious disease suffered by millions of children" (Schwartz).

Here is an example of a brief paraphrase of the same passage:

Although asthma and air pollution are often causally linked, there is much research showing that air pollution is not the chief cause of asthma and may in fact have no bearing on increased cases in the United States. Air pollution experts such as Joel Schwartz have suggested that environmentalists, politicians, and other regulators have blamed air pollution for asthma as a way of pushing their environmental agenda on law and policy. Because these people depend on environmental funding for their jobs, it makes sense they would want to blame as much on air pollution as possible. Yet in the case of asthma, the numbers simply don't add up.

2. *Use the information fairly.* Be careful to use supporting information in the way the author intended it. For example, it is unfair to quote an author as saying, "air quality dramatically worsened in Southern California" when he or she intended to say, "air quality dramatically worsened in Southern California during the 1980s, but thanks to the passage of important environmental legislation, improved greatly in the 1990s." This is called taking information out of context. This is using supporting evidence unfairly.

3. *Give credit where credit is due.* Giving credit is known as citing. You must use citations when you use someone else's information, but not every piece of supporting information needs a citation.

- If the supporting information is general knowledge—that is, it can be found in many sources—you do not have to cite your source.
- If you directly quote a source, you must cite it.
- If you paraphrase information from a specific source, you must cite it.

If you do not use citations where you should, you are plagiarizing—or stealing—someone else's work.

Citing Your Sources

There are a number of ways to cite your sources. Your teacher will probably want you to do it in one of three ways:

- Informal: As in the example in number 1 above, tell where you got the information as you present it in the text of your essay.
- Informal list: At the end of your essay, place an unnumbered list of all the sources you used. This tells the reader where, in general, your information came from.
- Formal: Use numbered footnotes. Footnotes are generally placed at the end of an article or essay, although they may be placed elsewhere depending on your teacher's requirements.

Works Cited

Schwartz, Joel. "Asthma and Air Pollution." American Enterprise for Public Policy Research 26 Sept. 2005.

Using MLA Style to Create a Works Cited List

You will probably need to create a list of works cited for your paper. These include materials that you quoted from, relied heavily on, or consulted to write your paper. There are several different ways to structure these references. The following examples are based on Modern Language Association (MLA) style, one of the major citation styles used by writers.

Book Entries

For most book entries you will need the author's name, the book's title, where the book was published, what company published it, and the year it was published. This information is usually found on the inside of the book. Variations on book entries include the following:

A Book by a Single Author
> Guest, Emma. *Children of AIDS: Africa's Orphan Crisis*. London: Sterling, 2003.

Two or More Books by the Same Author
> Friedman, Thomas L. *The World Is Flat: A Brief History of the Twentieth Century*. New York: Farrar, Straus and Giroux, 2005.
>
> ---. *From Beirut to Jerusalem*. New York: Doubleday, 1989.

A Book by Two or More Authors
> Pojman, Louis P., and Jeffrey Reiman. *The Death Penalty: For and Against*. Lanham, MD: Rowman & Littlefield, 1998.

A Book with an Editor
> Friedman, Lauri S., ed. *At Issue: What Motivates Suicide Bombers?* San Diego, CA: Greenhaven Press, 2004.

Periodical and Newspaper Entries

Entries for sources found in periodicals and newspapers are cited a bit differently than books. For one, these sources usually have a title and a publication name. They also may have specific dates and page numbers. Unlike book entries, you do not need to list where newspapers or periodicals are published or what company publishes them.

An Article from a Periodical
> Snow, Keith Harmon. "State Terror in Ethiopia." *Z Magazine* June 2004: 33–35.

An Unsigned Article from a Periodical
> "Broadcast Decency Rules." *Issues & Controversies on File* 30 Apr. 2004.

An Article from a Newspaper
> Constantino, Rebecca. "Fostering Love, Respecting Race." *Los Angeles Times* 14 Dec. 2002: B17.

Internet Sources

To document a source you found online, try to provide as much information on it as possible, including the author's name, the title of the document, date of publication or of last revision, the URL, and your date of access.

A Web Source

Shyovitz, David. "The History and Development of Yiddish." Jewish Virtual Library. 30 May 2005. www.jewishvirtuallibrary.org/jsource/History/yiddish.html. Accessed September 11, 2007.

Your teacher will tell you exactly how information should be cited in your essay. Generally, the very least information needed is the original author's name and the name of the article or other publication.

Be sure you know exactly what information your teacher requires before you start looking for your supporting information so that you know what information to include with your notes.

Appendix D

Sample Essay Topics

Air Pollution Is a Serious Problem

Air Pollution Is Not a Serious Problem

Water Pollution Is a Serious Problem

Water Pollution Is Not a Serious Problem

Mercury Pollution Is a Serious Problem

Mercury Pollution Is Not a Serious Problem

Chemical Pollutants Are a Serious Threat to Human Health

Chemical Pollutants Are Not a Serious Threat to Human Health

Air Pollution Causes Asthma

Air Pollution Is Not Responsible for the Increase in Asthma

Corporations Are Reckless Polluters

Corporations Comply with Environmental Regulations

Environmental Racism Endangers Minorities

Charges of Environmental Racism Are False

Environmentalists Overstate the Problem of Pollution

Environmentalists Help Protect the Environment for Everyone

Mercury in the Food Supply Causes Health Problems

Mercury in the Food Supply Does Not Pose a Health Risk

Herbicides and Pesticides Pose a Serious Health Risk

Herbicides and Pesticides Do Not Pose a Serious Health Risk

Americans Should Buy Organically Grown Produce to Avoid Ingesting Toxins

Organically Grown Produce Does Not Have Dietary Advantages

Tap Water Is Safe to Drink

Tap Water Is Not Safe to Drink

Bottled Water Is Less Polluted than Tap Water

Bottled Water Is More Polluted than Tap Water
Electronics Recycling Should Be Mandatory
Electronics Recycling Should Not Be Mandatory
Hydrogen Cars Can Reduce Air Pollution
Nuclear Energy Can Reduce Pollution
Nuclear Energy Will Create More Pollution
The Government Should Regulate Pollution
The Government Should Not Regulate Pollution
Carbon Credit Systems Help Reduce Pollution
Carbon Credit Systems Pass the Buck on Reducing Pollution

Organizations to Contact

American Council on Science and Health (ACSH)
1995 Broadway, Second Floor, New York, NY 10023 • (212) 362-7044 • fax: (212) 362-4919 • e-mail: acsh@acsh.org • Web site: www.asch.org

The American Council on Science and Health is a consumer education consortium concerned with, among other topics, issues related to the environment and health. The council publishes editorials, position papers, and books, including "The Mysterious Asthma Increase" and "Who Says PCBs Cause Cancer," which are available on its Web site.

The American Lung Association (ALA)
61 Broadway, Sixth Floor, New York, NY 10006 • (212) 315-8700 • Web site: www.lungusa.org

Founded in 1904 to fight tuberculosis, the American Lung Association (ALA) currently fights lung disease in all its forms, with special emphasis on asthma, tobacco control, and environmental health. Under the link "Air Quality" on its Web site, the ALA provides articles, fact sheets, and special reports on pollution-related issues, including its yearly "State of the Air."

Bluewater Network
311 California, Suite 510, San Francisco, CA 94104 • (415) 544-0790 • fax: (415) 544-0796 • e-mail: bluewater@bluewaternetwork.org • Web site: www.bluewaternetwork.org

The Bluewater Network promotes policy changes in government and industry to reduce dependence on fossil fuels and eradicate other root causes of air and water pollution, global warming, and habitat destruction. On its Web site the Bluewater Network publishes fact sheets on specific water pollution issues such as ship emissions, oil spills, and global warming. Articles available on the Web site include "Banishing Snowmobiles," "Super-Sized Cruise Ships Leave Wake of Wastes," and "Dirty Diesels."

Cato Institute

1000 Massachusetts Avenue NW, Washington, DC 20001 • (202) 842-0200 • fax: (202) 842-3490 • e-mail: cato@cato.org • Web site: www.cato.org

The Cato Institute is a libertarian public policy research foundation dedicated to limiting the role of government and protecting individual liberties. The institute publishes the quarterly magazine *Regulation* and the bimonthly *Cato Policy Report*. It disapproves of Environmental Protection Agency regulations, considering them too stringent. On its Web site the institute publishes many of its papers dealing with the environment, including "The Air Pollution Con Game," "Amending Superfund: Reform or Revamp?" and "Our Widespread Faith in Recycling Is Misplaced."

Clear the Air

1200 Eighteenth Street NW, Fifth Floor, Washington, DC 20036 • (202) 887-1715 • fax: (202) 887-8877 • e-mail: info@cleartheair.org • Web site: www. cleartheair.org

Clear the Air, which supports stricter air pollution controls, is a joint project of three leading clean air groups: the Clean Air Task Force, the National Environmental Trust, and the U.S. Public Interest Research Group (PIRG) Education Fund. On its Web site Clear the Air publishes news releases, fact sheets, and reports, including "Pollution on the Rise," "Fishing for Trouble: Mercury Is Making Our Nation's Fish Unsafe to Eat," and "Toxic Neighbors."

Competitive Enterprise Institute (CEI)

1001 Connecticut Avenue, NW, Suite 1250, Washington, DC 20036 • (202) 331-1010 • fax: (202) 331-0640 • e-mail: info@cei.org • Web site: www.cei.org

Competitive Enterprise Institute (CEI) is a public policy organization dedicated to the principles of free enterprise and limited government. The institute believes that consumers are best helped not by government regulation but by being allowed to make their own choices in a free marketplace and thus supports market-based pollution policies. On its Web site CEI publishes articles, editorials, speeches, and studies, including "Asthma, Roaches and Regulations," "Superfund Legislation: True Reform or a Hazardous Waste?" and "Foul Water or Foul Science? The EPA Targets America's Farms."

Earth Island Institute (EII)

300 Broadway, Suite 28, San Francisco, CA 94133 • (415) 788-3666 • fax: (415) 788-7324 • Web site: www.earthisland.org

Founded in 1982 by veteran environmentalist David Brower, Earth Island Institute (EII) develops and supports projects that counteract threats to the biological and cultural diversity that sustain the environment. Through education and activism, EII promotes the conservation, preservation, and restoration of the earth. EII publishes the quarterly, *Earth Island Journal*. Recent articles are available on the EII Web site, including "Breathless in Harlem," "Toxic Toast and Radioactive Raisin Bran," and "Cruise Ships Fail Pollution Tests."

Environmental Defense

Membership and Public Information • 1875 Connecticut Avenue, NW Suite 600, Washington, DC 20009 • (800) 684-3322 • e-mail: members@environmentaldefense.org • Web site: www.environmentaldefense.org

Environmental Defense, founded in 1967, works to protect the environmental rights of all people, including future generations, low-income communities, and communities of color. It focuses on U.S. environmental problems and the U.S. role in causing and solving environmental problems. Environmental Defense maintains an online archive of its articles, reports, press releases, and fact sheets, as well as resources for educators.

Environmental Protection Agency (EPA)

Ariel Rios Building, 1200 Pennsylvania Avenue NW, Washington, DC 20460 • (202) 272-0167 • Web site: www.epa.gov

The Environmental Protection Agency (EPA) is the federal agency in charge of protecting the environment and controlling pollution. The agency works toward these goals by assisting businesses and local environmental agencies, enacting and enforcing regulations, identifying and fining polluters, and cleaning up polluted sites. On its Web site EPA has links to specific pollution issues, including acid rain, the Clean Air Act, the Clean Water Act, hazardous waste, superfund, and recycling. Articles, memos, and speeches on a wide variety of pollution-related topics are available.

Friends of the Earth

1717 Massachusetts Avenue NW, Suite 600, Washington, DC 20036 • (877) 843-8687 • fax: (202) 783-0444 • e-mail: foe@foe.org • Web site: www.foe. org

Friends of the Earth is a national advocacy organization dedicated to protecting the planet from environmental degradation; preserving biological, cultural, and ethnic diversity; and empowering citizens to have an influential voice in decisions affecting the quality of their environment. It publishes the quarterly *Friends of the Earth*

Newsmagazine, recent and archived issues of which are available on its Web site.

GrassRoots Recycling Network (GRRN)

4200 Park Boulevard #290, Oakland, CA 94602 • Telephone and fax: (510) 531-5523 • Web site: www. grrn.org

GrassRoots Recycling Network's (GRRN) mission is to eliminate the waste of natural and human resources. The network advocates corporate accountability and public policies that eliminate waste and build sustainable communities. The GRRN Web site includes fact sheets, reports, and articles, including "Composting and Organics: Recycling vs. Bioreactors" and "Beyond Recycling: The Zero Waste Solution."

Greenpeace

702 H Street, NW, Washington, DC 20001 • (800) 326-0959 • (202) 462-1177 • e-mail: info@wdc.greenpeace. org • Web site: www.greenpeace.org

Greenpeace is an international nonprofit organization which accepts no funding from governments or corporations. Founded in 1971, it focuses on worldwide threats to the planet's biodiversity and environment, and directs attention to its mission through public acts of nonviolent civil disobedience. Greenpeace publishes technical reports, including "Man-made Chemicals in Maternal and Umbilical Cord Blood" and "Recycling of Electronic Waste in India and China."

Heritage Foundation

214 Massachusetts Avenue NE, Washington, DC 20002 • (800) 544-4843 • (202) 546-4400 • fax: (202) 544-6979 • e-mail: pubs@heritage.org • Web site: www.heritage.org

The Heritage Foundation is a conservative think tank that supports free enterprise and limited government. Its researchers criticize Environmental Protection Agency overregulation and believe that recycling is an ineffective method of dealing with waste. Its publications, such as the quarterly *Policy Review,* include studies on the uncertainty of global warming and the greenhouse effect. The articles "Keeping It Clean" and "Why the Government's CAFE Standards for Fuel Efficiency Should Be Repealed, Not Increased" are available on its Web site.

International Dark-Sky Association (IDA)

3225 North First Avenue, Tucson, AZ 85719 • (520) 293-3198 • fax: (520) 293-3192 • e-mail: ida@darksky. org • Web site: www.darksky.org

International Dark-Sky Association's (IDA) goals are to reverse the adverse environmental impact on dark skies by building awareness of the problem of light pollution and the solutions, including quality nighttime lighting. On its Web site IDA publishes fact sheets, slide shows demonstrating the impact of light pollution, and articles, including "Light Pollution: The Neglected Problem."

National Environmental Trust (NET)

1200 Eighteenth Street NW, Fifth Floor, Washington, DC 20036 • (202) 887-8800 • fax: (202) 887-8877 • e-mail: info@net.org • Web site: www.net.org

The National Environmental Trust (NET) is a nonprofit, nonpartisan organization established in 1994 to inform citizens about environmental problems and how they affect human health and quality of life. Its educational programs focus on clean air, global warming, energy, and other issues. NET publishes reports, fact sheets, and press releases.

National Recycling Coalition (NRC)

1325 G Street NW, Suite 1025, Washington, DC 20005
• (202) 347-0450 • fax: (202) 347-0449 • Web site:
www.nrc-recycle.org

The National Recycling Coalition (NRC) is a nonprofit organization dedicated to the advancement and improvement
of recycling, source reduction, composting, and reuse. It
provides technical information and education and advocacy services to recycling companies. NRC publishes tips
for spokespeople, including "How to Respond to Attacks
on Recycling in the Media" and "20 Press Release Ideas
to Promote Recycling."

Natural Resources Defense Council (NRDC)

40 West Twentieth Street, New York, NY 10011 • (212)
727-2700 • e-mail: proinfo@nrdc.org • Web site: www.
nrdc.org

The Natural Resources Defense Council (NRDC) is a nonprofit organization that uses law, science, and more than
four hundred thousand members nationwide to protect
the planet's wildlife and wild places and to ensure a safe
and healthy environment for all living things. On its Web
site NRDC provides links to specific pollution-related topics such as clean air and energy, global warming, clean
water and oceans, and toxic chemicals and health. Fact
sheets, reports, and articles, including "The Campaign
to Dump Dirty Diesel," "Pollution from Giant Livestock
Farms Threatens Public Health," and "Pesticides Threaten
Farm Children's Health" are available.

Physicians for Social Responsibility (PSR)

1875 Connecticut Avenue NW, Suite 1012, Washington,
DC 20009 • (202) 667-4260 • fax: (202) 667-4201 •
e-mail: psrnatl@psr.org • Web site: www.psr.org

Founded in 1961, Physicians for Social Responsibility
(PSR) documented the presence of strontium-90—a

highly radioactive waste product of atmospheric nuclear testing—in American children's teeth. This finding led rapidly to the Limited Nuclear Test Ban treaty that ended above-ground explosions by the superpowers. PSR's mission is to address public health threats that affect people in the United States and around the world. The PSR Web site publishes fact sheets and article excerpts, including "Healthy Fish, Healthy Families" and "Asthma and the Role of Air Pollution."

Political Economy Research Center (PERC)
502 South Nineteenth Avenue, Suite 211, Bozeman, MT 59718 • (406) 587-9591 • fax: (406) 586-7555 • e-mail: perc@perc.org • Web site: www.perc.org

The Political Economy Research Center (PERC) is a non-profit research and educational organization that seeks market-oriented solutions to environmental problems. Areas of research covered in the PERC Policy Series papers include endangered species, forestry, fisheries, mines, parks, public lands, property rights, hazardous waste, pollution, water, and wildlife. PERC conducts a variety of conferences, offers internships and fellowships, and provides environmental education materials. On its Web site PERC provides access to recent and archived articles, reports, and its policy series, including such titles as "Property Rights and Pesticides" and "Superfund: The Shortcut That Failed."

Sierra Club
85 Second Street, Second Floor, San Francisco, CA 94105 • (415) 977-5500 • fax: (415) 977-5500 • e-mail: information@sierraclub.org • Web site: www. sierraclub.org

Founded in 1892, the Sierra Club is the oldest and largest grassroots environmental organization in the United States. Its mission is to help people explore, enjoy, and protect the wild places of the earth and practice and promote the responsible use of the earth's ecosystems and resources. The Sierra Club publishes books, calendars, newsletters, blogs, and a bimonthly print magazine, *Sierra*.

Union of Concerned Scientists (UCS)

2 Brattle Square, Cambridge, MA 02238 • (617) 547-5552 • fax: (617) 864-9405 • Web site: www.ucsusa.org

Union of Concerned Scientists (USC) is an independent nonprofit alliance of concerned citizens and scientists, founded in 1969 by faculty members and students at the Massachusetts Institute of Technology who were concerned about the misuse of science and technology in society. It sponsors the Sound Science Initiative, through which scientists provide information on environmental science to government and the media. USC publishes an annual report, and posts on its Web site information about global environment, clean vehicles, clean energy, and other issues.

Worldwatch Institute

1776 Massachusetts Avenue NW, Washington, DC 20036 • (202) 452-1999 • fax: (202) 296-7368 • e-mail: worldwatch@worldwatch.org • Web site: www.worldwatch.org

Worldwatch Institute is a nonprofit public policy research organization dedicated to informing policy makers and the public about emerging global problems and trends and the complex links between the world economy and its environmental support systems. It publishes the bimonthly *World Watch* magazine, the Environmental Alert series, and several policy papers. Recent and archived issues of *World Watch* are available on its Web site.

Bibliography

Books

Jon Ayres, Robert L. Maynard, and Roy Richards, *Air Pollution and Health*. Singapore: World Scientific Publishing, 2005.

Dave Brummet and Lillian Brummet, *Trash Talk: An Inspirational Guide to Saving Time and Money Through Better Waste and Resource Management*. Baltimore: PublishAmerica, 2004.

David Burnie, *Endangered Planet*. Boston: Kingfisher, 2004.

Tony Clark, *Inside the Bottle: An Expose of the Bottled Water Industry*. Ottawa: Polaris Institute, 2005.

Marla Cone, *Silent Snow: The Slow Poisoning of the Arctic*. New York: Grove Press, 2005.

E. Melanie DuPuis, *Smoke and Mirrors: The Politics and Culture of Air Pollution*. New York: New York University Press, 2004.

Kaitlen Jay Exum and Lynn Messina, eds., *The Car and Its Future*. New York: H.W. Wilson, 2004.

Alexandra Fix, *Glass*. Portsmouth, NH: Heinemann, 2007.

Rodney M. Fujita, *Heal the Ocean: Solutions for Saving Our Seas*. Gabriola Island, BC: New Society Publishers, 2003.

Roy A. Gallant, *Atmosphere: Sea of Air*. New York: Benchmark Books, 2003.

George A. Gonzalez, *The Politics of Air Pollution: Urban Growth, Ecological Modernization, and Symbolic Inclusion*. New York: State University of New York Press, 2006.

Jack M. Hollander, *The Real Environmental Crisis: Why Poverty, Not Affluence, Is the Environment's Number One Enemy.* Berkeley: University of California Press, 2004.

J.S. Kidd and Renee A. Kidd, *Air Pollution: Problems and Solutions.* New York: Facts On File, 2005.

H. Jeffrey Leonard, *Pollution and the Struggle for the World Product: Multinational Corporations, Environment, and International Comparative Advantage.* London: Cambridge University Press, 2006.

Carl N. McDaniel, *Wisdom for a Livable Planet.* San Antonio: Trinity University Press, 2005.

Joseph J. Romm, *The Hype About Hydrogen: Fact and Fiction in the Race to Save the Climate.* Washington, DC: Island Press, 2004, revised edition 2005.

Elizabeth Royte, *Garbage Land: On the Secret Trail of Trash.* Boston: Little, Brown, 2005.

Joel Schwartz, *No Way Back: Why Air Pollution Will Continue to Decline.* Washington, DC: AEI Press, 2003.

Nicky Scott, *Reduce, Reuse, Recycle.* Devon, UK: Green Books, 2007.

Kenneth M. Vigil, *Clean Water: An Introduction to Water Quality and Pollution Control.* Corvallis: Oregon State University Press, 2003.

Carl A. Zimring, *Cash for Your Trash: Scrap Recycling in America.* New Brunswick, NJ: Rutgers University Press, 2005.

Periodicals

American Lung Association, "Health Effects of Ozone and Particle Pollution." In *State of the Air 2005,* American Lung Association, 2005.

Douglas H. Benevento, "Facing Up to Future Smog: Controlling Pollution More Difficult than 30 Years Ago," *Denver Post,* June 20, 2004.

Mark Bernstein and David Whitman, "Smog Alert: The Challenges of Battling Ozone Pollution," *Environment*, October 2005.

Steve Bollard, "Tap Water Misconceptions Fuel Bottled Water Sales," *Daily Orange Online*, April 15, 2004.

Tom Christopher, "Turf Wars," *House and Garden*, August 2004.

Alan Pell Crawford, "Trouble on Tap: What's Really in Your Water?" *Vegetarian Times*, June 2004.

Sophia Cruz, "Hydrogen Cars: The Solution to Transportation, Pollution and Energy," *Associated Content*, September 5, 2005.

Keay Davidson, "Road to Hydrogen Cars May Not Be So Clean: Environmental Peril in Making, Containing Fuel," *San Francisco Chronicle*, December 20, 2004.

Sheila Davis, testimony to the Senate Subcommittee on Superfund and Waste Management, Environment and Public Works Committee, July 26, 2005. www.epw.senate.gov/109th/Davis_testimony.pdf.

Gregg Easterbrook, "Clear Skies, No Lies," *New York Times*, February 16, 2005.

Rene Ebersole, "Is Your Drinking Water Safe?" *National Wildlife*, June–July 2004.

David Fink, "Making Mercury Matters Worse," *National Wildlife*, April–May 2004.

Michael Fumento, "Cleaner Air Brings Dirtier Tricks," *Tech Central Station*, July 9, 2004. www.techcentralstation.com.

Dana Joel Gattuso, "Mandated Recycling of Electronics: Creating a Mountain out of a Landfill," *Monthly Planet*, April 30, 2005.

Elizabeth Grossman, "Them's the Breaks," *Grist.com*, June 29, 2006. www.grist.org/advice/books/2006/06/29/grossman.

Jackie Gubeno, "New Kid in Town: The Emergence of Hybrid-Fueled Cars Could Boost the Number of Nickel-Metal Hydride Batteries in the Recycling Stream," *Recycling Today,* January 2005.

Corinna Kester, "Diesels Versus Hybrids: Comparing the Environmental Costs," *World Watch,* July–August 2005.

Melissa Knopper, "Clearing the Air," *E: The Environmental Magazine,* July–August 2005.

Sally Kuzemchak, "Should You Buy Organic?" *Parents,* April 2005.

Frannie A. Leautier, "Urban Air Pollution Management," World Bank Institute, November 2003. www1.world-bank.org/devoutreach/nov03/article.asp?id = 218.

Ben Lieberman, "New York Summer Without New York Smog?" *New York Post,* September 15, 2004.

Barbara Loecher, "Is Your Water Fit to Drink?" *Prevention,* April 2004.

Cheryl Long, "Hazards of the World's Most Common Herbicide," *Mother Earth News,* October–November 2005.

Erica Lumiere, "Fish: Healthy or Toxic?" *Harper's Bazaar,* May 2004.

Margaret Magnarelli and Peter Jaret, "Is Your Family's Water Safe?" *Good Housekeeping,* February 2005.

Alex Markels and Randy Dotinga, "Don't Go in the Water," *U.S. News & World Report,* August 16, 2004.

David Martosko, "Mercury Risk? Scares Mislead American Consumers," *Milwaukee Journal-Sentinel,* August 12, 2006.

Barbara McClintock, "Beware the Pesticide Scare," *TheTyee.ca,* April 27, 2004.

Katharine Mieszkowski, "Mercury Rising," *Salon.com,* April 18, 2005. www.salon.com.

Susan Milius, "Foraging Seabirds Carry Contaminants Home," *Science News*, July 16, 2005.

Steven Milloy, "Pesticides Not a Threat to Students," *FoxNews.com*, August 9, 2005.

National Review, "Polluted Thinking," July 25, 2006.

Keith Naughton, "Hybrid Nation? Nope," *Newsweek*, October 10, 2005.

Robert Rio, "Mercury: Grain of Truth, Gram of Nonsense," *Heartland Institute*, March 1, 2004. www.heartland.org.

Joel Schwartz, "Asthma and Air Pollution," American Enterprise Institute for Public Policy Research, September 26, 2005.

Wendy Munson Scullin, "Keep Off the Grass! The Modern American Lawn Is a Chemical Nightmare, but Alternatives Abound," *E: The Environmental Magazine* 16, no. 3 (May–June 2005).

Andy Simmons and Richard Sacks, "Clean Machines," *Reader's Digest*, April 2004.

Gina Solomon, Elizabeth H. Humphreys, and Mark D. Miller, "Asthma and the Environment: Connecting the Dots," *Contemporary Pediatrics* 21, no. 18 (August 2004).

Vernon Stent, "Throwing Away the Throw-Away Culture," *EzineArticles*, September 7, 2005. http://ezinearticles.com/?Throwing-Away-the-Throw-Away-Culture&id = 69046.

Richard Truett, "Automakers Think Green," *Automotive News*, November 1, 2004.

Jim Wooten, "Ignore Gloom: Environment Will Survive," *Atlanta Journal-Constitution*, April 19, 2005.

Yan Zhan, "China's Groundwater Future Increasingly Murky," WorldWatch Institute, November 28, 2006. www.worldwatch.org/node/4753/print.

Web Sites

Beach Clean Ups (www.beachcleanups.org). This site was started by students at High Tech High Media Arts and provides information on beach cleanups in the San Diego area. Students can be contacted to advise on how to start cleanup activities in communities around the United States.

A Better Earth Project (www.abetterearth.org). A project of the Institute for Humane Studies at George Mason University, this is a nonprofit educational organization that promotes innovative thinking about how to achieve a peaceful, prosperous, and pollution-free world. Its goal is to encourage students to think critically about the successes and failures of the environmental movement. The project sponsors a Web site, a summer seminar, and an e-mail newsletter.

Cato Institute: Environment and Climate (www.cato.org/research/nat-studies/index.html). The Cato Institute is a conservative think tank that seeks to protect the environment without sacrificing economic liberty. The Web site includes a reading list with articles promoting libertarian approaches to environmental protection and skepticism about environmentalist claims.

Environmental Protection Agency (www.epa.gov). The Environmental Protection Agency is a government organization charged with protecting human health and the environment. The agency's Web site contains fact sheets, speeches, reports, and other information regarding pollution in the United States.

Recycling Revolution (www.recycling-revolution.com). Contains a wealth of information about recycling and recycling programs.

Truthout Environment (http://truthout.org/environment. shtml). A reader-supported site that provides links to recent news stories and opinion pieces on environmental issues, including ways the U.S. government and large corporations contribute to pollution and global warming. Offers a free e-mail subscription.

Index

Pictures Credits

Cover: © Louie Psihoyos/Corbis

AP Images, 8, 11, 15, 18, 24, 27, 32, 36, 40, 43, 46, 50, 53, 50

About the Editor

Lauri S. Friedman earned her bachelor's degree in religion and political science from Vassar College in Poughkeepsie, NY. Her studies there focused on political Islam. Friedman has worked as a non-fiction writer, a newspaper journalist, and an editor for more than 7 years. She has accumulated extensive experience in both academic and professional settings.

Friedman has edited and authored numerous publications for Greenhaven Press on controversial social issues such as gay marriage, Islam, energy, discrimination, suicide bombers, and the war on terror. Much of the *Writing the Critical Essay* series has been under her direction or authorship. She was instrumental in the creation of the series, and played a critical role in its conception and development.